About Island Press

Island Press is the only nonprofit organization in the United States whose principal purpose is the publication of books on environmental issues and natural resource management. We provide solutions-oriented information to professionals, public officials, business and community leaders, and concerned citizens who are shaping responses to environmental problems.

In 2000, Island Press celebrates its sixteenth anniversary as the leading provider of timely and practical books that take a multidisciplinary approach to critical environmental concerns. Our growing list of titles reflects our commitment to bringing the best of an expanding body of literature to the environmental community throughout North America and the world.

Support for Island Press is provided by The Jenifer Altman Foundation, The Bullitt Foundation, The Mary Flagler Cary Charitable Trust, The Nathan Cummings Foundation, The Geraldine R. Dodge Foundation, The Charles Engelhard Foundation, The Ford Foundation, The Vira I. Heinz Endowment, The W. Alton Jones Foundation, The John D. and Catherine T. MacArthur Foundation, The Andrew W. Mellon Foundation, The Charles Stewart Mott Foundation, The Curtis and Edith Munson Foundation, The National Fish and Wildlife Foundation, The National Science Foundation, The New-Land Foundation, The David and Lucile Packard Foundation, The Pew Charitable Trusts, The Surdna Foundation, The Winslow Foundation, and individual donors.

Designing
Sustainable
Communities

Designing Sustainable Communities

Learning from Village Homes

Judy Corbett and Michael Corbett

Foreword by
Robert L. Thayer

ISLAND PRESS
Washington, D.C. ♦ Covelo, California

Library of Congress Cataloging-in-Publication Data
Corbett, Judy.
    Designing sustainable communities : learning from Village Homes / Judy Corbett and Michael N. Corbett ; foreword by Robert L. Thayer.
        p.   cm.
    Includes bibliographical references and index.
    ISBN 1–55963–686–6
    1. Planned communities. 2. Real estate development—Environmental aspects.
    3. Land use—Planning. 4. Sustainable development. I. Corbett, Michael N.
    II. Title.
    HT169.55.C67   2000
    307.1'216—dc21   99–052419
                                                                             CIP

Printed on recycled, acid-free paper

Printed in Canada.
10 9 8 7 6 5 4 3

Contents

Foreword

I am standing in the rain atop an earth-sheltered solar house in the community of Village Homes in Davis, California, while dark-suited executives of Japan's Takenaka Corporation and their interpreter climb the wooden steps to the landscaped roof. Their limousine and driver wait in the parking lot fifty yards to the south. We huddle under umbrellas and I speak slowly, allowing the translator to communicate my words into Japanese—how the house's roof is covered with eight inches of soil, native ground cover, and shrubs; how its owners have never paid even one nickel to the local utility company for power to heat or cool it; how BTU for BTU, it is probably the most energy-efficient house in northern California; how the owners built it with their own hands.

I am talking to executives of Japan's premier architecture and construction company, builders of the Kansai International Airport, the Tokyo Dome, and so many versions of high-rise apartment and office buildings that they refer to them by model number (D-3, A-5, etc.). These gracious guests have decided to visit California, and in particular Village Homes, to understand the swelling movement toward sustainable development that has captured many of the minds and not just a few hearts of the American planning, design, and development community. As a long-standing Village Homes resident, university professor, designer, and sustainable development researcher myself, I gladly undertake this public service, which when analyzed with any forethought probably does far more good than any five lectures to sleepy sophomores.

My guests thank me from under their umbrellas. We bow to each other in accordance with the Japanese custom; they give me the traditional Japanese gift plus some brochures of their impressive urban accomplishments, reenter their limousine, and depart. I walk back among the fruit trees beside the freshly flowing storm-water drainage swales on the greenbelt paths to my house in the northern section of Village Homes.

I have given countless such tours—still undoubtedly far fewer than my friends Michael and Judy Corbett, authors of this book and creators of this most amazing and important place. But I never tire of it, and each time it has become easier until now the ideas and words emerge seemingly of their own will. It is my small labor of love, dwarfed in scale when compared with the effort expended by Michael and Judy to bring this extraordinary community into existence. But since 1976, when I first moved in, I have watched the community grow and mature, helping it along with a tiny nudge or two of my own. What a joy it has been to live in a place where I can practice at home what I teach at the university: less energy expenditure, more water conservation, more community, less driving, more bike riding, less alienation and loneliness, more kids' play, more interaction with neighbors. Each of us, it seems, longs to live in a manner that reconciles our deepest inner convictions with external reality. I love this place, and for that I welcome the chance to introduce this book.

The name *Village Homes* has perhaps an ordinary ring to it, as if any builder might choose it as a modest name for a new subdivision, complete with colored flags (there were never any of those here!). But Village Homes is at once both ordinary and extraordinary: ordinary in that it is a genuine, much-loved home to several hundred people, many of whom (myself included) would never seriously consider living anywhere else; extraordinary in that it is one of the best examples of multifunction sustainable development in the world. Here, we are all accustomed to walking tours of visitors, from regional to statewide to international, roaming the pedestrian paths, engaging us in conversation, and taking pictures of what to us are really quite ordinary, but very good, lives.

What makes this place special? Michael and Judy will inform you, the reader, of this in detail in the chapters that follow. For all its fame and significance and for all the magazine, radio, and television features about Village Homes that have been published and produced in U.S. and international media, there is still the need for a good book that places the contribution of Village Homes in the context of contemporary planning, design, and development theory and practice. Here is such a book. Perhaps the most important contribution of Village Homes as a real place—and of this book as a significant contribution to the literature—is that Village Homes and the ideas behind it have never lost their relevance in a quarter century of existence. Buzzwords such as *solar age, appropriate technology, sustainability, new urbanism,* and *smart growth* have come and in many cases gone, but this community keeps on serving as the reality anchor to each. Here, in the Yolo clay loam soil outside these solar houses, is the "real deal" that persistently exemplifies and illustrates the reasons why humanity must continue the written and spoken dialog on a better way to plan, design, and live on the earth.

Let Michael and Judy tell you the details of Village Homes and enframe the newest directions in the design of socially and ecologically responsible communities. They are the experts: Michael consults worldwide, and Judy is the spark behind the well-respected Local Government Commission in Sacramento, California. Let me, however, tell you a few more personal details about our home place. In the final analysis, an ecological community such as Village Homes must be much more than a laboratory for testing new planning theories—it must be a *home* to those who live there. As I look back over my twenty-two years of residence, my mind floods with pleasant memories: of Sunday evening potlucks on the small greenbelt outside our home, with multi-age pickup stickball and volleyball games; of our teenage children skimboarding across the retention ponds after a heavy spring rain; of the explosion of residents onto the greenbelt and pathways when the fresh Delta breeze blows after a hot summer day; of my proud moments explaining the solar and water-conserving features of my house to classes of students; of the group photograph of Village Homes teenagers who had just graduated from Davis Senior High School; of shaking down and bagging almonds at the annual Village Homes almond harvest; of picking luscious white peaches off the landscape trees after a summer swim at the community pool; of early-days bragging rights over whose utility bill was smallest; of first noticing Lacey, my future wife, while singing at a Village Homes potluck in 1976; of rejecting lucrative faculty positions at other institutions because I couldn't stand the idea of leaving Village Homes.

Perhaps the most salient measure of the success of this place as an example of where sustainable development has been and where it ought to go is the simple fact that Michael and Judy Corbett *live here* (as in *live* with a capital *L*). How many developers live in the subdivisions they plan and build? As if to add the final keystone in the arch of the community they created, Michael opened the Plumshire Inn, a small five-star restaurant in the heart of the community center. Nestled among modest solar office buildings reminiscent of a French village and set against the natural drainage swale and community vegetable gardens, the Plumshire Inn has become the jewel in the crown of our community center. It was not enough for Michael to build a world-renowned solar community and become a well-known ecological planner; he is now also a superb maître d' who talks to every guest who walks through the door, counseling them on wines and occasionally giving away a dessert if his customers wait too long for an entrée to emerge from the kitchen. He is solely responsible for making it impossible for me to tolerate bad wine!

My Village Homes sustainable development tours for students and professionals now often end at Plumshire, where I introduce them to Michael. When Lacey and I eat at Plumshire and walk the greenbelt paths back to our house in the evening, we marvel at our good fortune to have found ourselves living where we do. The path home takes us past the best any community can offer: beautiful, well-loved, energy-efficient solar houses; community vineyards, orchards, and vegetable gardens; water-conserving landscapes; children playing away from traffic; birds singing and nesting; neighbors talking to one another. Even the village dogs seem to know how good they've got it and seldom fight. *These* are the sustaining measures of community, and it is this essential synthesis that Michael and Judy extrapolate from Village Homes into the future of sustainable development in this book. As the authors, they speak with the authority of seasoned experience, but in this foreword, I have the delicious opportunity to speak spontaneously from the heart. I just love this place!

No, we won't sell you our house—we're never leaving!

Robert L. Thayer, FASLA
Village Homes
July 14, 1999

Preface

When we set out to design and build Village Homes in 1972, it seemed unlikely that we would be successful. We had no financial assets and no track record in development. We were embarking on a large-scale project that incorporated numerous untried and innovative features. The most likely outcome, and the one we expected, was that we would not succeed but would be able to publish a book about our experiences and describe how a forward-looking community could be designed. Our planning concepts and design ideas might then be useful to others.

Luck was on our side. It took a great deal of tenacity and perseverance, but in the end we were able to overcome multiple obstacles and build Village Homes.

Our first book describing Village Homes and its design philosophies, titled *A Better Place to Live,* was published by Rodale Press in 1981. Now, more than twenty-five years after the start of Village Homes, we are writing another book in an attempt to pass on our planning ideas, some of what we learned from building Village Homes, and information about other projects and people who are making an earnest effort to create a truly sustainable way of living on this planet.

We can only hope that both the living example of Village Homes and the information offered in this book will assist those who are attempting to move away from the environmentally destructive and socially inappropriate trends that have produced the vast majority of homes and communities over the past half century—and that still dominate the way society is built today. We hope the reader will accept the planning strategies we provide not as a blueprint to follow but as an inspiration to those who are willing to break away from the current, environmentally unfriendly way of building and help chart a new course to sustainability.

Acknowledgments

We thank and appreciate those who have contributed to our efforts in writing this book. Invaluable editorial and writing assistance was provided by Jean Lamming, Nicole Brashear, Karen Fowler, and Dana Matalon. Our son, Christopher Corbett, formatted the photographs. The influence of John Klein, whose eloquence so enhanced *A Better Place to Live,* can be found in this renewed effort to describe Village Homes and the thinking that inspired it.

In chapter 4, Kevin Wolf contributed his valuable insight as well as research for the section addressing water. Rob Weiner assisted us with accuracy and content in the section on housing, and Lyra Halprin provided the same help with the section addressing agriculture. Lyra, a neighbor who has raised her family in Village Homes, and her family have been an important source of support in other ways as well.

Peter Asmus offered his abundant literary and research capabilities in writing much of chapter 5. For chapter 10, we must thank John Lawick, Bill McDonough, Vicky Ranney, John Clark, and Victor Dover for their help in providing information and photographs. We also appreciate their contributions in building on the Village Homes experiment to bring it to the next step.

For his inspiration and support, we thank Robert Sommer. He has believed in this project since the beginning. And we thank the many Village Homes residents, Rob and Lacey Thayer included, who have over the years made our home a wonderful community and a supportive place to raise a family.

Acknowledgments

Chapter 1

From Piecemeal Planning to Sustainable Development

Over the past half century, the concentric growth pattern of cities in the United States has produced urbanization in the form of an incoherent sprawl of look-alike residential subdivisions, commercial strips, big-box retailers, and commercial and industrial parks, all physically isolated from one another. At the same time, we have experienced continually increasing traffic congestion and air pollution, a result of the dependence on the automobile created by this inefficient land use pattern. Perhaps even more discouraging is the rapid conversion of forest, farmland, and open space accompanying the sprawl, which is outpacing population growth by factors of three to fifteen.[1]

Urban sprawl is causing our inner cities and first-ring suburbs, many of which were at one time examples of good planning, to deteriorate. Minnesota legislator Myron Orfield, in his book *Metropolitics,* documented a doubling of the number of poor and minority children in inner-city schools in the Minneapolis–St. Paul region during the 1980s. Seventy-eight new schools were built in newer suburbs while 162 urban and older suburban schools were shut down.[2]

No longer is there the human-scale development that in the past provided physical beauty, a sense of community, and a setting where basic human needs can be fulfilled. Instead, urbanization, coupled with much of our modern technology, has produced a society and lifestyle that are unhealthy and stressful for the individual. At the same time, this lifestyle is systematically destroying the earth's support systems.

Unfortunately, those responsible for land use planning have not often considered the natural environment when making decisions. For the most part, neither have they considered the subtle sociopsychological needs of

Typical U.S. automobile-oriented commercial sprawl. (Photograph courtesy of Local Government Commission)

Sprawling, monolithic housing in a suburban area.

people. They have focused instead on the cities' physical systems, short-term economic considerations, and the interests of the development community. In 1974, scientist and philosopher René Dubos pointed out:

> Planners are primarily concerned with the technological efficiency of the urban system with regard to industrial, economic and political activities. They pay less attention to the psychological and emotional needs of city dwellers or to the relationship between city life and civilization. While the technological aspects of the urban system are fairly well understood and can be manipulated, little is actually known about the influence that cites have exerted on the development of human potentialities and therefore on the emergence of civilized life. Civilizations have flourished in cities for more than 5,000 years, but they have difficulty in surviving the huge urban agglomerations of the contemporary world.[3]

A great deal of what we have been doing wrong can be summed up in the term *piecemeal planning*. Piecemeal planning is the result of our tendency to try to deal with each problem as if it existed in a vacuum, as if our attempts to deal with it had no effect on other values and problems. Our suburban neighborhoods provide an instructive and unfortunate example. For the past quarter century, they have generally been laid out with no more than two or three goals in mind: to provide every family with its own house and yard, connected to water, sewer, gas, and electric utilities; to allow every resident to drive speedily through the neighborhood to his or her own front door; and to exclude any kind of commercial enterprise.

Having achieved these goals, we have discovered a host of new problems. There is no local community because there are no local shops or public areas where we meet our immediate neighbors—only private houses and private yards and the wide, inhospitable streets. Children rarely see adults at work. Any errand requires the use of a car, and then the streets are clogged with traffic and it is difficult to find a parking place. In many communities, children cannot get anywhere safely without being chauffeured. Large amounts of gasoline are consumed, and automobile exhaust pollutes the air. Storm runoff from streets and roofs causes erosion, flooding, and damage downstream. Sewage disposal becomes a problem rather than producing a usable by-product, even though fertilizer for agriculture is increasingly costly.

Unenlightened and undaunted, we have tackled these problems in the same piecemeal fashion, creating whole new sets of problems. We have installed antipollution devices on cars, but that has decreased gas mileage. We have built suburban shopping centers with huge parking lots and huge ponds to contain storm runoff, and now we notice that agricultural land and open space are getting scarce—and so on, indefinitely.

There is a pattern here: at each step, we have neglected to look at the whole picture. We have assumed that our wealth, technology, and "problem-solving ability" can bail us out of any new problem somewhere down the road. But technology and ingenuity have not bailed us out. In fact, we find ourselves deeper and deeper in a quagmire of environmental and social problems. As Milwaukee's mayor, John Norquist, once said to us, "A lot of our problems are caused by solutions."

Long before the 1940s, there were visionaries who saw looming problems in uncontrolled concentric growth around cities and were promoting alternatives. In 1898, social reformer Ebenezer Howard promulgated a scheme to build new towns rather than add population to the already large cities. Called the garden city plan, Howard's scheme would have incorporated a unified system of community landownership, greenbelts, and a balance of land uses, including industry and housing for workers, a balance between industrial and residential uses, self-government, and an intimate relationship between city and countryside. As Howard pictured it, "each inhabitant of the whole group, though in one sense living in a town of small size, would

The town center in Letchworth, England, remains full of vitality nearly a century after this garden city was built.

be in reality living in, and would enjoy all the advantages of a great and most beautiful city; and yet all the fresh delights of the country."[4] A series of small, self-sufficient towns was to be interconnected through a mass transit system, with a cultural center located at the core. As a result of Howard's writings and influence, two garden cities were built in England: Letchworth, begun in 1903, and Welwyn Garden City, established in 1920.

During the early 1920s, a group of about twenty-five individuals joined together to further Howard's concept. The group held a common belief that the existing centralized, profit-oriented metropolitan society should be replaced with a decentralized one made up of environmentally balanced regions. Called the Regional Planning Association of America, the organization sought to locate people outside cities, arguing for "a dedication to a new social order where people have decent homes, a stable community life, a healthy and varied environment, and a genuinely urban culture."[5] The organization's membership included such people as planning critic Lewis Mumford and Clarence Stein, who was chief architect of Radburn, New Jersey, one of the few substantial attempts at garden city development in the United States. The group dissolved in the early 1930s, having been involved in the development of Sunnyside, a neighborhood community in New York composed of houses grouped around open space owned by a community association, and Radburn, built in New Jersey. Radburn continued the Sunnyside land use pattern on a larger scale, bringing together a series of Sunnyside-like neighborhoods, each centered on an elementary school and a shopping center. The automobile was deemphasized in both of these plans, which used cul-de-sacs as the only access to the homes. A network of paths provided pedestrians with direct access to all destinations in the community.[6]

Although political and economic forces prevented full realization of the vision of the members of the Regional Planning Association, the garden city model was not forgotten, and it served as inspiration for subsequent new-town developments. In 1936, right after the Great Depression, the administration of President Franklin D. Roosevelt built three garden city communities: Greenbelt, Maryland; Greenhills, Ohio; and Greendale, Wisconsin. Other communities built on the garden city pattern include Columbia, Maryland, and Reston, Virginia—and many more in Europe. These can be visited today and stand as living proof of the value of the garden city as a means of providing people with a better living environment.

Researchers recently compared Almere, a new town in the Netherlands based on the garden city pattern, and the new town of Milton Keynes, England, where the neighborhood development pattern was rejected in favor of the "choices" provided by automobile-oriented development. The

The garden city of Greendale, Wisconsin, features houses facing narrow streets.

In Greendale, homes overlook a greenbelt and paths.

A path leads from housing to the commercial area of Greendale.

researchers concluded, "Not only is it in the interests of energy conservation and environmental planning to develop towns like Almere, rather than Milton Keynes, but they are also popular with the inhabitants, an important factor not always considered by planners and other urban gatekeepers."[7] For this reason, the garden city concept will be referred to continually throughout this book as a better model for community planning.

Although the memory of Ebenezer Howard and his garden city concept has faded, a number of new revelations not only reinforce the validity of Howard's ideas but also, if viewed together, form the basis for a new, broader vision of planning. Best named *sustainable design,* this vision includes both environmental and social considerations. Although the term *sustainability* is currently used in a variety of contexts, we believe that a sustainable community is one that allows its inhabitants to live in a way that does not damage the environment or consume nonrenewable resources. At the same time, a sustainable community supports the realization of human potential.

Individuals from various pursuits have contributed insights. One is economist E. F. Schumacher, who in the subtitle of his book *Small Is Beautiful* succinctly expressed his philosophy: "economics as if people mattered."[8] Another is Howard Odum, whose work has played a major role in the development of the field of ecology.[9] Edward T. Hall's *The Hidden Dimension*[10] and Robert Sommer's *Personal Space*[11] and *Social Design,*[12] which explore the relationships of the human-made environment with the individual and society, catalyzed the development of a new academic endeavor, environmental psychology. This combination of economics, ecology, psychology, and sociology has become the backbone of a body of knowledge about the relationship between humans and the environment. The students of this interdisciplinary field have been a strong force in bringing about an awareness of the earth, people, and their interrelatedness.

During the 1970s, the concept of sustainable community design gained momentum. Though unsophisticated and many times misused, the environmental impact statement (EIS) or environmental impact report (EIR), required by most governmental agencies before approval of many projects, is an example of a significant change in process aimed at examining the potential effects of development. As for products, the most visible examples are those created by work in three distinct areas. The first of these areas was the movement toward environmentally benign sources of energy, for which Amory Lovins argued eloquently in his book *Soft Energy Paths*.[13] The second was the development and adoption of different forms of organic agriculture, as advocated years ago by J. I. Rodale and described in *Organic Gardening* magazine. The third was the attempt in the 1970s to build ecologically planned communities. These included Cerro Gordo, near Cottage Grove, Oregon; Solar Village, planned by California architects Sim van der Ryn and Peter Calthorpe but never built; and our own Village Homes neighborhood in Davis, California, which was heavily influenced by the garden city movement. Of these planning experiments, Village Homes—the focus of this book—has proven the most successful, having achieved build-out and met its twin goals of helping people live more lightly on the land and creating a sense of community.

The changes brought about by the administration of President Ronald Reagan in the 1980s put most progress on hold, however, and the problems of urban development worsened. Interest in producing better development all but disappeared. Between 1980 and 1990, the conversion of forest, farmland, and open space to sprawled residential and commercial development accelerated. Toxic chemicals accumulated in the environment at an increasing rate. The earth's protective ozone layer continued to be depleted. Global warming became recognized as a scientific reality, rain forests continued to be cut and lost at an alarming rate, more nuclear waste was accumulated, and more agricultural land was lost to salinization and erosion as well as to urbanization. The distribution of wealth became more lopsided, and social problems such as drug addiction and crime increased.

The decade of the 1990s, however, brought hope for the future. There was again a growing concern about environmental problems throughout the world and renewed enthusiasm and commitment to improving community design and building sustainable communities.

One promising movement, the British Urban Villages Campaign, started up in late 1989 with the support of the prince of Wales. The mission of the campaign is to bring about more livable urban environments. Characteristics of the British urban village are generally described as follows:

- A resident population of 3,000–5,000 in an area of about forty hectares[14]
- Medium-density land use, ensuring that all parts of the village are within walking or bicycling distance
- A diverse range of mixed land uses at neighborhood, block, street, and building levels
- Convenient shopping and services and local recreational and community facilities
- A high quality of urban design and architecture
- An employment base that encourages residents to work in the local center or from home
- An energy- and information-efficient built environment that is responsive to climate, location, and orientation
- Human-scale urban design that encourages crime prevention and home-care networks
- Diverse and usable public spaces
- Integrated land use and transportation design
- A pedestrian- and bicycle-friendly, traffic-calmed environment
- A mixture of public and private housing providing for a range of needs and incomes
- An urban form that reinforces economic, social, and environmental sustainability
- A management system that ensures long-term achievement and maintenance of the urban village concept

The British Urban Villages Campaign engages in public education and supports development that meets its basic criteria. Members have promoted urban villages on large inner-city brownfield sites (previously utilized properties that may or may not suffer from toxic contamination), on suburban and urban peripheries, on infill sites (unused properties within the existing urban area), and on greenfield sites (properties outside the urban area that have never been built on). In 1996, they could point to thirteen such projects in England, either completed or on the drawing board, that generally followed their principles. At the national policy level, the group is receiving considerable support.[15]

A parallel movement in the United States, called the new urbanism or livable communities movement, has been primarily driven by public dissatisfaction with faceless sprawl development and the loss of a sense of place experienced in many communities throughout the country. It has resulted in a proliferation of books and magazine and newspaper articles that once again examine the way we build and the alternative paths we could take. Although this movement has a positive influence on environmental sustainability, its principal focus is on creating human-scale neighborhoods and towns designed to better meet the social needs of people.

The construction of a little resort community in Florida called Seaside was key to creating the new urbanism or livable communities movement in the United States. Andres Duany and Elizabeth Plater-Zyberk were the architects of the project. They joined with developer Robert Davis in creating an eighty-acre village for 2,000 residents based on house designs and site plans heavily influenced by communities of the early 1900s. Their new community, which broke ground in 1981, includes a post office, a school, a general store, and other retail services placed on narrow streets within walking

The community of Seaside, Florida, prophesied a new movement in urban planning. (Photograph courtesy of DPZ Architects and Town Planners)

distance of homes with front porches. Located on a stunning beach, the community was conceived primarily as a vacation retreat. However, it achieved widespread public attention because of its innate appeal to the media, social critics, and the general public. The project revealed people's longing for traditional, small-town amenities and their dissatisfaction with the psychological and sociological effects of urban sprawl.

On the other side of the country, a similar movement was going on—but this one was aimed primarily at reducing traffic jams and dependence on automobiles. *The Pedestrian Pocket Book,* edited by architect Doug Kelbaugh, encouraged the creation of neighborhoods at light-rail stops that link with one another and with existing urban centers. These "pedestrian pockets" are designed as little urban villages with a mix of housing, shopping centers, community facilities, and employment and with all buildings within a short walk of the transit station.[16]

The notion of pedestrian pockets was quickly embraced, and a cross-fertilization occurred between the movements on the East Coast and the West Coast. In Los Angeles, Playa Vista, designed in 1989 by a team that included local architects Elizabeth Moule and Stefanos Polyzoides as well as Duany and Plater-Zyberk, was a major urban infill project consisting of more than 1,000 acres. The project organized a sequence of higher-density neighborhoods with a system of streets, open spaces, and parks and a village center containing residential, retail, and civic uses. The plan included a low-emission internal shuttle system that was to be linked to regional transportation systems. The Laguna West mixed-use neighborhood of 3,499 units in Sacramento, California, designed in 1990 by architect Peter Calthorpe, also made use of the community design of Seaside as well as the pedestrian pocket concept.

During the same period in Sacramento, California, the Local Government Commission, a nonprofit, membership, policy-development organization of mayors, city council members, and county supervisors of which Judy Corbett, one of the authors of this book, is executive director, set out to develop guidelines for local officials on reducing automobile use and associated air pollution through better land use planning. With a grant in 1990 from the California Air Resources Board, the organization began work on a manual that would provide local policy makers with proven alternatives to urban sprawl, based on the actual success of Village Homes and Seaside. At the urging of Peter Katz, who was then working on a book titled *The New Urbanism,*[17] we invited Peter Calthorpe, Elizabeth Plater-Zyberk, Andres Duany, Elizabeth Moule, and Stefanos Polyzoides to our home for dinner. The group was told they were to spend the evening with us developing a new vision for elected officials of what communities of the future should be—a positive alternative to urban sprawl. Together with attorney Steve Weissman, we worked out a set of fifteen community principles that described this new concept in a very precise manner. Because the group agreed that no community exists in isolation, we decided we should also develop a set of regional principles. Finally, because Judy's goal was to provide this information to elected officials, who would need to know exactly how to set these ideas in motion, the group developed a set of steps for implementing them.

The principles were unveiled before 100 California mayors, city council members, and county supervisors at the fall 1991 conference of the Local Government Commission, held at the Ahwahnee Hotel in Yosemite National Park. It was a watershed weekend. Many of those present had already advocated limited growth in their cities—but lightbulbs were switched on in the politicians' heads. Here was a win-win solution! There *is* a way for communities to grow without being destroyed; maybe growth could even make them better!

Several elected officials at the conference immediately picked up the ideas and implementation strategies and went home to carry them out. Among them was Rick Cole, then the mayor of Pasadena. Under his leadership, the city of Pasadena embraced the idea that it should be a place where people can get around without a car. Within a year, citizens of this anti-growth city voted to adopt a general plan that focuses new growth in mixed-use neighborhoods located near transit stops.

Because of the site of their unveiling, the principles were dubbed the Ahwahnee Principles. They have been published and distributed throughout the United States. According to *Western City* magazine, a publication of the League of California Cities, more than 100 cities and eighteen counties in the state had by early 1997 adopted some or all of the Ahwahnee Principles in their general plans.[18] The principles, presented in the accompanying box, have influenced the pattern of new development, urban revitalization, and infill development in cities as diverse as Reno, Nevada, and the small community of Oakdale in California's San Joaquin Valley.

The Ahwahnee Principles bring together the aesthetic and social concerns of Duany and Plater-Zyberk, Calthorpe's focus on transportation and regional issues, and our own broader ecological concerns—to the mutual satisfaction of all the authors. It is remarkable how closely these principles reflect Howard's original garden city concept.

There was, however, one major point of disagreement among ourselves and the rest of the architects. The majority felt strongly wedded to gridded

The Ahwahnee Principles

Preamble:

Existing patterns of urban and suburban development seriously impair our quality of life. The symptoms are: more congestion and air pollution resulting from our increased dependence on automobiles, the loss of precious open space, the need for costly improvements to roads and public services, the inequitable distribution of economic resources, and the loss of a sense of community. By drawing upon the best from the past and the present, we can plan communities that will more successfully serve the needs of those who live and work within them. Such planning should adhere to certain fundamental principles.

Community Principles:

1. All planning should be in the form of complete and integrated communities containing housing, shops, work places, schools, parks and civic facilities essential to the daily life of the residents.
2. Community size should be designed so that housing, jobs, daily needs and other activities are within easy walking distance of each other.
3. As many activities as possible should be located within easy walking distance of transit stops.
4. A community should contain a diversity of housing types to enable citizens from a wide range of economic levels and age groups to live within its boundaries.
5. Businesses within the community should provide a range of job types for the community's residents.
6. The location and character of the community should be consistent with a larger transit network.
7. The community should have a center focus that combines commercial, civic, cultural and recreational uses.
8. The community should contain an ample supply of specialized open space in the form of squares, greens and parks whose frequent use is encouraged through placement and design.
9. Public spaces should be designed to encourage the attention and presence of people at all hours of the day and night.
10. Each community or cluster of communities should have a well-defined edge, such as agricultural greenbelts or wildlife corridors, permanently protected from development.
11. Streets, pedestrian paths and bike paths should contribute to a system of fully-connected and interesting routes to all destinations. Their design should encourage pedestrian and bicycle use by being small and spatially defined by buildings, trees and lighting; and by discouraging high speed traffic.
12. Wherever possible, the natural terrain, drainage and vegetation of the community should be preserved with superior examples contained within parks or greenbelts.
13. The community design should help conserve resources and minimize waste.
14. Communities should provide for the efficient use of water through the use of natural drainage, drought tolerant landscaping and recycling.
15. **The street orientation, the placement of buildings and the use of shading should contribute to the energy efficiency of the community.**

The Ahwahnee Principles (*Continued*)

Regional Principles:

1. The regional land-use planning structure should be integrated within a larger transportation network built around transit rather than freeways.
2. Regions should be bounded by and provide a continuous system of green-belt/wildlife corridors to be determined by natural conditions.
3. Regional institutions and services (government, stadiums, museums, etc.) should be located in the urban core.
4. Materials and methods of construction should be specific to the region, exhibiting a continuity of history and culture and compatibility with the climate to encourage the development of local character and community identity.

Implementation Principles:

1. The general plan should be updated to incorporate the above principles.
2. Rather than allowing developer-initiated, piecemeal development, local governments should take charge of the planning process. General plans should designate where new growth, infill or redevelopment will be allowed to occur.
3. Prior to any development, a specific plan should be prepared based on these planning principles.
4. Plans should be developed through an open process and participants in the process should be provided visual models of all planning proposals.

Source: Local Government Commission Web site: http://www.lgc.org/clc/ahwahnee/principles.html

streets. We, on the other hand, follow the garden city concept—that street layout should depend on local circumstances, as long as all destinations can be reached directly by bicycle or pedestrian path.

We used a cul-de-sac design in building Village Homes because we could not have developed the natural drainage system, common areas, and off-street bike paths without using dead-end streets. This system also allowed us to pave less land, leaving more space for agricultural production. A recent survey by American LIVES Inc., a market research firm, showed that although a majority of people like most of the attributes of the new urbanism, they also prefer living on a cul-de-sac.[19] As long as direct paths are available for pedestrians and bicyclists, we believe cul-de-sacs to be an acceptable and often advantageous design option.

There was a second important outgrowth of the 1991 Local Government Commission conference, in addition to the successful unveiling of the

Ahwahnee Principles. The architects who spoke at the conference decided that because their work was not getting the recognition and respect it deserved within their own profession, they should work together to create a new architectural movement. Duany and Plater-Zyberk subsequently took the lead, organizing the first conference of the Congress for the New Urbanism (CNU) in 1993. With the focused efforts of Katz, Calthorpe, Moule, and Polyzoides and the help of the Energy Foundation and others, the original group of architects, joined by architect Dan Solomon, incorporated as a formal nonprofit educational organization. The original six then expanded to become fifteen, including a number of board members who are not architects, including Judy. The CNU's annual congress has become an increasingly popular event, and the organization now has a staff, a membership of more than one thousand, myriad volunteers, and a number of projects in progress.

A charter was drafted and signed in 1996. Its principal authors included the authors of the Ahwahnee Principles, with the exception of Michael Corbett. The charter embraces the idea of restoring and reconfiguring existing development before building on open land, as articulated in the second paragraph of the accompanying box.

During the early 1990s, stimulated by the new urbanism movement, a

---

CNU Charter

The Congress for the New Urbanism
views disinvestment in central cities, the spread of placeless sprawl, increasing separation by race and income, environmental deterioration, loss of agricultural lands and wilderness, and the erosion of society's built heritage as one interrelated community-building challenge.

We stand
for the restoration of existing urban centers and towns within coherent metropolitan regions, the reconfiguration of sprawling suburbs into communities of real neighborhoods and diverse districts, the conservation of natural environments, and the preservation of our built legacy.

We recognize
that physical solutions by themselves will not solve social and economic problems, but neither can economic vitality, community stability, and environmental health be sustained without a coherent and supportive physical framework.

CNU Charter (Continued)

We advocate

the restructuring of public policy and development practices to support the following principles: neighborhoods should be diverse in use and population; communities should be designed for the pedestrian and transit as well as the car; cities and towns should be shaped by physically defined and universally accessible public spaces and community institutions; urban places should be framed by architecture and landscape design that celebrate local history, climate, ecology, and building practice.

We represent

a broad-based citizenry, composed of public and private sector leaders, community activists, and multidisciplinary professionals. We are committed to reestablishing the relationship between the art of building and the making of community, through citizen-based participatory planning and design.

We dedicate

ourselves to reclaiming our homes, blocks, streets, parks, neighborhoods, districts, towns, cities, regions and environment.

Source: From the CNU Charter adopted May 3–5, 1996, in Charleston, South Carolina.

---

number of walkable new urbanist developments were proposed in California, Oregon, and Washington, and many were proposed in Florida and at other sites on the East Coast. Some, such as Fairview Village near Portland, Oregon, developed by Holt & Haugh, Inc., are well on their way to completion; others, such as Playa Vista in Los Angeles, have been slow in coming to fruition. The *New Urban News* reported in 1998 that 201 new urbanist projects were completed or in the planning stages.[20] This is a conservative estimate because it does not include infill projects.

In practice, none of the new urbanist developments planned or built to date address ecological concerns beyond the very important problem of reducing dependence on the automobile. However, Elizabeth Moule and Stefanos Polyzoides, cofounders of the CNU, have been retained to work on a new, energy-efficient development in Tuscon, Arizona—Civano, a community modeled in part after Village Homes. Some members of the CNU also are pushing the organization to comprehensively address a broad base of environmental concerns.

The CNU has had a major influence on national policy. The U.S.

Department of Housing and Urban Development in 1996 developed guidelines for the expenditure of grants and loans to turn blighted neighborhoods into thriving neighborhoods. These guidelines are modeled after new urbanist principles: points are awarded to projects that have a compact size based on a comfortable walking distance from the center; a mix of compatible uses such as housing, shops, workplaces, parks, and civic and cultural institutions; a mix of housing types to accommodate a range of incomes, ages, and lifestyles; energy-efficient buildings with compatible architectural variety; a public gathering space at the center such as a square, green, or public building; a network of interconnecting, pedestrian-friendly streets, alleys, and blocks that encourage links to adjacent neighborhoods; a connection to mass transit; and neighborhood edges defined by boulevards, greenbelts, or other natural features.[21]

New urbanist concepts are also reflected in the Smart Growth initiative spearheaded by the Environmental Protection Agency, a program that reaches out to local governments, environmentalists, transportation experts, and the development community working through the Urban Land Institute, the International City/County Management Association, the National Association of Counties, the Local Government Commission, the CNU, and numerous other organizations.

The work of the Urban Land Institute advocating "smart growth" through transportation planning, increased housing density, state and regional growth policies, and inner-city redevelopment has been an important contribution to the progress of new urbanism. Large-scale developers and builders must change their ways if significant improvements are to be made in the design of the built environment. The Urban Land Institute's recent publications and conferences and its general support of smart growth are of critical importance.[22]

The broader concept of sustainable development also picked up momentum in the 1990s. Books were once again published on the subject, including Sim Van der Ryn and Stuart Cowan's *Ecological Design*,[23] Robert Thayer's *Gray World, Green Heart: Technology, Nature, and Sustainable Landscape*,[24] and Timothy Beatley and Kristy Manning's *The Ecology of Place: Planning for Environment, Economy, and Community*.[25] Reid Ewing's *Best Development Practices: A Primer for Smart Growth*, published by the American Planning Association,[26] and *Green Development: Integrating Ecology and Real Estate*, written by the staff of the Rocky Mountain Institute,[27] take the concepts from theory to practice.

In some places, local governments and businesses began taking action.

Colorado's governor, Roy Romer, launched a program in 1994 to give awards for environmentally sensitive development. In 1995, the Home Builders Association of Metropolitan Denver started the first Built Green program, modeled on the Green Building Program in Austin, Texas, to certify claims of environmentally sound construction. Since then, 1,200 homes—about 5 percent of production in the populous six-county Denver region—have been "built green."[28]

Significantly, this issue has received attention at the highest levels of government. During his first term in office, President Bill Clinton established the President's Council on Sustainable Development," made up of a broad cross section of business and environmental interests. The council has been focusing on stimulating cities and counties to follow the lead of communities such as Chattanooga, Tennessee, where public and private efforts have led to cleaner air, cleaner water, a revitalized city center, more regional cooperation, and a stronger economy.[29]

Results of the November 1998 election sent a profound message to politicians as well as builders and developers. More than two hundred initiatives were on ballots nationwide to stop sprawl and save open space, and most of them won.

Vice President Al Gore kicked off 1999 by unveiling a series of programs to help local governments build "places where young and old can walk, bike, and play together."[30] A number of governors were promoting "livable communities" or smart growth, including Republican governor Christine Todd Whitman of New Jersey, and members of the United States Congress formed a caucus for livable communities led by Congressman Earl Blumenhauer, formerly a member of the Portland City Council.

Finally, the 1990s saw a very hopeful trend for leaders in the business community to step forward and say that a better environment is good for the economy. The Bank of America was among the first businesses to do so.[31] It was followed by such groups as the Sierra Business Council, a group of business leaders from the Sierra Nevada mountain range in California, and Joint Venture: Silicon Valley Network, an organization of businesses in the computer industry in and around the San Francisco Bay Area.

These leaders also placed new emphasis on the need for planning at the regional level. A study of land use and the California economy undertaken by the Center for Continuing Study of the California Economy identified regions as the critical geographic unit for organizing land use decisions in California.[32]

Although piecemeal planning still characterizes the way most development is carried out today, the signs of the 1990s point to increasing interest from environmentalists, business leaders, developers, and government to find a more comprehensive, more sustainable approach to planning and building communities. We hope that this is only the beginning of a movement that will fully blossom in the twenty-first century.

Chapter 2

An Introduction to Village Homes

Growing up in Village Homes gave me a sense of freedom and safety that would be difficult to find in the usual urban neighborhood. The orchards, swimming pool, parks, gardens, and greenbelts within Village Homes offered many stimulating, exciting, joyful places for me to play with my friends. We could walk out our back doors into greenbelts full of all kinds of trees to climb with fruit to eat and gardens with vegetables to nibble on. Even when we were very young, the network of greenbelts allowed my friends and I to go anywhere in the community without facing the danger of crossing a street. This experience has shaped the way I see American communities. Now that I am no longer living in Village Homes, I feel locked in by the fence in my backyard and the street in front of my house. I feel a loss of the freedom I had as a child.

—Christopher Corbett

Located in a university town, Davis, California, Village Homes is a sixty-acre, 242-unit mixed-use residential "garden village" incorporating innovative ecological and social features. It is an effort of the 1970s toward sustainable development inspired by the garden city. Because it is a neighborhood, it is referred to as a garden village. The layout of the community allows all homes to face south to maximize use of the sun for heating. Homes—accommodating people from a variety of income levels—use passive or active solar space heating and have rooftop solar water heaters. The streets, really just alleys, are long cul-de-sacs and are far narrower than streets in standard housing developments. The houses open onto common areas linked by bicycle paths that form a grid throughout the neighborhood. Agricultural land is incorporated throughout. A natural drainage system takes

The children of Village Homes, a garden village in Davis, California.

care of runoff through a system of creeks and ponds. The inclusion of parks, recreational opportunities, a day-care facility, and a commercial center all add up to a community where residents can enjoy a higher quality of life while living lightly on the land.

More than just one of the best examples in the world of sustainable development built to date,[1] Village Homes is also a wonderful place to raise children. The idea for Village Homes came about before our son, Christopher, now twenty-four, was born, and he was therefore able to grow up there.

Our first child, Lisa, was born when Michael was a student in the architecture program at California State Polytechnic College in San Luis Obispo. Having been heavily influenced by our three years there as student and student-wife, we believed that our mission in life was to design beautiful spaces for people to live in. Later, after working for an architect in San Francisco, Michael began designing and building very attractive but very energy-consuming homes, some with flat roofs and large, west-facing windows, including two residences for ourselves.

A return to college changed both our perspectives and our lives. Judy enrolled in the master's program in ecology at the University of California, Davis, and Michael took classes in ecology at Sacramento State University while working toward a degree in psychology. We learned that the beautiful but energy-consuming houses we had been building were not what the

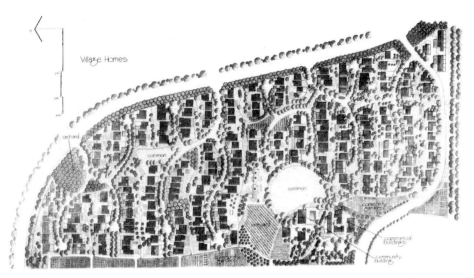

A map of Village Homes.

world needed. We learned that the world's ecology was not healthy, that the supply of oil was not limitless, and that nuclear power was not an answer to society's energy needs because there is no safe way to store the waste. We also became aware that the prevailing pattern of neighborhood planning was undermining people's sense of community.

Early in the 1970s, we began to meet with a group of friends, primarily graduate students, to plan our own community that would address the ecological and social problems of the day. The meetings were advertised in the local newspaper and were open to the public. We called ourselves "the Village." Eventually, some thirty people were involved, meeting every Wednesday night to discuss what a community ought, ideally, to be.

The discussion centered on a shared sense of dislocation, disconnection, and powerlessness and on a concern for the environment. We wondered whether it would be possible to recover some of the homier aspects of village life within the context of the modern neighborhood. We believed it should be possible to design a community so that one might live more lightly on the land. The possibility of starting a school was discussed, along with various communal agricultural schemes and the need for neighborhood celebrations and festivals.

More than a year later, when the community had been designed and we were looking for land to buy, the Village group disbanded. We had not agreed on a site; many had not been able to raise the necessary investment capital, and their parents were not about to loan them money for such a crazy scheme; and we had not been able to work out a compromise between the more radical and less radical members. Some had decided they really did not want to make a long-term commitment to living in Davis. But the process had given us a chance to listen to new ideas as well as to think through some of our own desires and philosophies about building a more socially satisfying and resource-efficient neighborhood.

We determined to move ahead with the Village ourselves, as a commercial venture. Although we viewed as a long shot our chances of making such enormous changes to traditional development, we thought it was worth a try. At least we would be able to write a book about our attempt to create a better place to live and the institutional barriers that stood in the way.

In 1972, Michael found an infill property in the westernmost part of Davis. Because the Davis City Council had placed a moratorium on growth, we were able to option the land from the anxious owner-developer. The price was $6,000 per acre, and a $10,000 down payment was all that was required initially. Michael began designing a prospectus and trying to interest local investors in the project.

The timing of all this was no coincidence. Also in Davis during that period, another group was putting together a celebration called Whole Earth Day. Whole Earth Day has since become an annual local festival of dance and music, crafts and cooking, alternative energy innovations and architectural design. It both created and was the result of a growing public concern for the environment.

A third and critical factor leading to the realization of Village Homes was the Davis City Council election. In 1971, a group made up mostly of students, many of them fellow students in the Graduate Group in Ecology at the University of California, Davis (one of the country's first such programs), began meeting to discuss how the Davis community might address the serious ecological problems facing the country. We called ourselves the Greater Davis Planning and Research Group. Among the proposals developed by the group at our regular Sunday night potlucks was that of stopping urban sprawl and preserving agricultural land. We also proposed reducing the area devoted to streets and parking lots downtown and opening up that land for higher-density development. We suggested that growth in the city should be halted while the city reviewed and updated its general plan through a process of research and public involvement.

One member of the group, Robert Black, a former student body president at the university, agreed to run for membership on the city council, using the programs of the Greater Davis Planning and Research Group as a platform. There were three vacant seats to be filled that year on the five-member council. In the last weeks of the election, our platform was embraced by two additional candidates, an environmental health professional who worked for the university and an attorney who would be the first woman elected to the council. All three were elected, taking over majority control from the previously conservative city council. Council members rapidly began to implement the many innovations they had promised the voters, including a moratorium on all growth until the city's general plan could be rewritten.

The Village Homes proposal embodied many of the ideas of the new general plan and reflected the philosophy of the new city council. Even so, a massive effort was required to gain city approval for the innovative features of our Village Homes plan. The council did so over the objections and against the recommendations of the city staff. The staff objected to the narrowness of the streets, the inward-facing houses, and the long cul-de-sacs. The spacing of the houses, closer than usual to the street and to one another, was in violation of the standard rules for subdivisions. Moreover, the city planning director did not believe that agriculture would be compatible with housing. The fire and police chiefs objected to the layout and worried about access for emergency vehicles. As for natural drainage, one city planner said that we were attempting to move back in time to some date well before the Industrial Revolution. In fact, the only element we remember as having caused no controversy was the decision to emphasize drought-resistant plants.

The city staff recommended nonapproval and asked us to revise the plan, eliminating all the controversial features. Instead, we chose to argue our plan point by point before the city council. We credit a colleague, writer John Klein, for most of the work on this. Klein was wonderful at dissecting the staff's critiques and arguing against them persuasively. Even so, it is a rare city council that is willing to go against the recommendations of its staff. Fortunately, our city council members were willing to think "outside the box."

One sticking point was the natural drainage system. In the beginning, city engineers were hesitant to approve it. As a compromise, the city council asked that we post a bond for funds to install a traditional drainage system if our "radical" one proved to be a failure. Several years into construction of the project, we experienced a severe storm. Streets all over Davis were flooded, but not those in Village Homes. In addition, city water backed into our drainage channels and we successfully absorbed not only our own rainwater but also some from other neighborhoods. Our system had no problem with leaves clogging drains, and our land had been graded in such a manner that a large quantity of water was held in channels, never reaching our roads or homes. On the basis of this experience, the city did not stipulate that we post a bond for the remaining phases of construction.

Another problem area for city staff was the width of our proposed streets. We found ourselves at loggerheads with the fire department, who feared that they would be unable to reach the homes in the event of a fire. They agreed to an experiment, joining us in a large parking lot with two fire trucks and traffic cones. They told us exactly what they needed to be able to do—park two fire trucks side by side and open the inside doors to allow the drivers to exit. We measured the space required to provide for their needs. Most of our streets were wide enough, but some were not. Council member Robert Black came up with a compromise—provision of a three-foot easement on each side of the street. This measure gained quick approval from the city council.

The entire process taught us that change must originate with local elected officials. Howard Reese, Davis's city manager at that time, noted that "staff people have a tremendous investment in doing things the same way as they did them yesterday." He remembered the process as an educational one for everyone involved.[2] The issues raised by the Village Homes plan were new to city staff members, he recalled. They could not speak to the issues as experts. Instead, they had to become problem solvers, and the transition took a little time. In all, the process of approval took two and a half years.

We actually needed this delay in order to raise the money required. The initial investment of $130,000 was raised relatively easily from family members and friends at $10,000 per share. This was enough to option the land, but additional capital was required for construction.

We took the development proposal, written in such a way as to emphasize the ecological advantages of the subdivision, to thirty-two banks and savings and loan institutions in the Sacramento area and the San Francisco Bay Area. Every financial institution declined to give us a loan. The Bank of America's refusal was particularly explicit. The bank was not turning down the loan because of the economic risks involved, representatives told us. They simply found the project's philosophies distasteful.

We changed our approach and rewrote the proposal, describing the innovations as nothing new, just ideas lifted from other successful projects. We asked for a loan only to fund the infrastructure of the first unit and did not mention future plans for some of the more communal aspects of the neighborhood. Michael took the new proposal to a savings and loan where his parents, who were builders, were good customers, and we finally got the loan we needed. By Thanksgiving of 1975, the big work—roads and grading and the like—was done and the first houses were under construction.

Soon, the first greenbelt was landscaped and the homes were on the market. Solar technology was very new at this time, and local real estate agents knew little about it and trusted it less. They actively discouraged prospective buyers, disparaged the experimental features of the project, and raised concerns about resale value. We heard that Village Homes was the laughingstock of the local realty community.

The houses went on sale during a period of recession. Sales were bad all over, but the houses in Village Homes sold in spite of the real estate agents and the recession. Within a year, work began on the second unit, and this time it was clear that the project would be a financial success. The savings and loan financed the remaining four units without any hesitation.

Completing the entire project took six more years. In the beginning, housing prices in Village Homes were comparable to prices elsewhere in Davis, and they were a bargain at that because of their money-saving solar features. However, at this writing, calculated by the square foot, Village Homes is the most expensive place in Davis in which to buy—homes there cost $11 per square foot more than the average house in Davis. This is due less to the houses themselves—they were built at the modest end of the housing scale—and more to the neighborhood, which is seen as a very desirable place to live. The homes come on the market less frequently than do homes in other areas of Davis, and they sell twice as quickly. Because of the higher cost of housing, they are often bought by families wealthier than the original owners. Many houses are currently being expanded and remodeled.

The Innovations of Village Homes

We chose the design features that make up Village Homes to either enhance the social life of the community or create a more sustainable environment; however, many features accomplish both purposes. In fact, in the planning stages, we knew we had hit upon a design innovation that was "right" whenever it supported more than one of our goals. For instance, narrowing the streets saved money and resources; made the streets safer by slowing traffic; used less land, making more available for other purposes, such as food production; reduced urban runoff; kept the neighborhood cooler in summer by absorbing less heat; and increased the sense of community by making it easier to say hello to the neighbors when taking off for work in the morning. Although getting these innovations through the required layers of government and financing them was extremely difficult—we were challenging business as usual, and innovators are rarely appreciated—the end result has proven well worth the time and trouble. The innovations—adding up to a design that allows a sense of community to develop and promotes water and energy conservation, use of solar energy, walking and biking, and a lifestyle that is closer to nature—have added up to a successful venture in development, whether judged from an economic, a social, or an ecological perspective.

COMMUNITY

Although it has received less public attention than the energy-saving innovations, the sense of community seems to be what residents like best about Village Homes. We began working to develop a sense of community from the very beginning. During the construction phase, many features of the subdivision were built by those who had already moved in. This allowed residents to get acquainted with their neighbors in a natural, purposeful way and had the added benefit of keeping costs down. Work parties were organized to build the community swimming pool, the pool complex, play structures, the bridges that cross our creeks, and the community center.

Some residents participated in the design of their own homes, and a few

A Village Homes work party.

even served as owner-builders. A group of students were given the opportunity to build their own nine-bedroom housing cooperative.

We were looking to create a neighborhood with a diverse population. Thus, the development includes twenty apartments that rent at prices comparable to those of others in Davis, and the homes range from 600-square-foot common-wall homes to 2,800-square-foot detached dwellings. Our goal was to make sure that 16 percent of our homes went to low-income homeowners, and we had an innovative plan for achieving this. Construction jobs were offered to several interested migrant farmworkers and to a family of immigrants from Pakistan. It was hoped that as part of the crew, the workers would learn construction skills and develop the experience and expertise to pursue other employment opportunities when the project ended. In addition, after a year's employment, we gave workers the chance to build their own homes under the supervision of a job foreman, using their labor as the down payment on a house in the community. Time has proven that low-income families can become an integral part of the community.

Features of the subdivision encourage a continued sense of community. There are no through streets. Paths are the quickest way to travel through the neighborhood, and they encourage more energy-efficient modes of transportation: walking or biking. The paths simultaneously promote community

Bicycle paths in Village Homes assist community interaction.

orientation by creating a place for neighbors to meet and interact. Frequently, neighbors stop to talk with one another on their way to communal areas such as the swimming pool, the community center, and the playing field.

The narrow streets allow a greater sense of community ownership to develop because residents perceive the space as belonging to them rather than being a no-man's-land. Thus, neighbors feel justified in signaling to slow a speeding car. Because the streets all dead-end, parents feel relaxed about letting their children use them for skateboarding.

Initially, critics were concerned that the community would be physically isolated from the rest of the city, that it would be like a gated community; however, this fear has not been realized. The bike paths of Village Homes serve children and parents from adjacent areas who pass through on their way to work or school, and residents of other Davis neighborhoods frequently use our paths for jogging or strolling. Their children play on our playing fields.

Two large grassy areas or miniparks in the development are often the site of community potlucks, birthday parties, soccer games, and the like. These spaces provide places and reasons to get to know one's neighbors that the typical housing development sorely lacks.

A Village Homes potluck on the green.

In addition to the parks, the use of which all residents share, smaller common areas are shared by only the eight homes that border them. In the beginning, we did some basic landscaping in these areas and then gave the residents surrounding each one $600 to make their own personal improvements as a group. Many planted fruit trees, some created vegetable gardens, and a few planted lawns, created fire pits, or built children's play structures. Today, maintaining this smaller common area is a cooperative responsibility among the bordering houses, requiring contact and agreement. Although it is possible to buy off the responsibility of maintenance for an additional $30 per month in fees, to date only one homeowner has chosen to pay this fee, a nonresident owner whose property is occupied by renters.

Residents in some of these eight-house sets have developed strong social ties, frequently sharing child-care responsibilities and vacations. Others have chosen to be more private, simply maintaining the common area with occasional interaction. Community participation is not mandatory in Village Homes, although by design the opportunity is there for all residents. Indeed, one can be a private person and enjoy living in Village Homes.

Recently, a graduate student compared friendship patterns in Village Homes with those in a nearby neighborhood. The survey revealed that Village Homes residents knew an average of forty neighbors, compared with seventeen in the standard development, and had three or four close friends in the neighborhood, compared with one in the control group. Residents of Village Homes also spend more time socializing in their own neighborhood. Thus, even though it is possible to remain anonymous in the community, many residents choose to take advantage of the opportunity to form friendships.

A part of the emphasis on community in Village Homes is embodied in the Village Homeowners' Association. People in the United States often feel powerless with regard to political issues, and this powerlessness expresses itself as inertia when they face the more personal and immediate issues of their public lives. By creating a polity even smaller than the city, Village Homes returns to people a larger measure of control over their lives. Every resident in Village Homes automatically belongs to the homeowners' association, a democratic community association. Monthly fees cover maintenance of the parks, agricultural land, swimming pool, and community center. Every resident has an equal vote in issues that concern the community, though participation is in no way mandatory. It is perfectly possible and quite common for individuals to live in Village Homes and not be politically involved, just as this option is a popular one in other communities.

The homeowners' association is headed by a board of five directors, elected annually from the community and receiving no compensation. The directors hold an open monthly meeting and also meet irregularly as needed. Two additional boards are appointed by the directors of the association. These are the Architectural Review Board, which reviews all construction and remodeling plans (within thirty days, or approval is automatic), and the Agricultural Board, which organizes and oversees use of the agricultural lands.

There is one other board whose members are elected. The Plumshire Corporation is a subsidiary corporation owned by the homeowners' association. The community elects six residents to the Plumshire Board of Directors, and a seventh director serves or an appoitment from the Village Homes board. The Plumshire Corporation owns three office buildings in the Village Homes subdivision, a small restaurant, and a dance studio, which are rented almost exclusively to residents. It also has a majority interest in ten apartment units in Village Homes. The income is used to reduce residents' monthly fees. These fees, in 1999, were set at $83 per month and continue to rise with inflation, though not at the same pace. Although our income-producing property is helping to keep the fees low, we believe that the joint ownership of land is even more important in that it gives people a place and a reason to come together, thereby allowing a sense of community to develop.

ENERGY CONSERVATION AND USE OF SOLAR ENERGY

Much of the national and international interest in Village Homes has been a result of the community's emphasis on energy conservation, especially its solar energy features. The Village Homes development is a widely recognized example of conservation with a high standard of comfort and convenience.

The Davis climate is Mediterranean. Temperatures on summer days often exceed 100 degrees Fahrenheit, but nights are usually cool. Winters are mild and freezes are rare, although fog and rain can last for weeks. The solar approach in individual houses in Village Homes ranges from active mechanical systems to simple passive systems. In some ways, Village Homes has served as a laboratory for solar energy technology, including earth-covered houses and active heating systems, but some of the most successful strategies have been the simplest.

Making careful use of insulation was one of the first steps we took in reducing energy demand in our homes. Walls and roofs are well insulated, and windows are double paned. All cracks are sealed. Sills are set in mastic to reduce leakage. Caulking is done around doors and windows where cracks are left between the rough frame and the finished window or door frame.

A passive solar house in Village Homes.

The interior of a passive solar house with skylights in Village Homes.

The edges of the slab floors are also insulated to retain heat in winter and coolness in summer. We chose light-colored exterior walls and roofs to reflect the sun and keep the houses cooler. Light-colored tile is used for roofing in most of the homes.

Houses in Village Homes are designed to store the sun's heat by means of high-mass materials. The massive adobe walls of the old California missions are a classic example of this principle. The adobe absorbs and stores heat and coolness to bring temperature extremes within the comfort zone. Other materials able to store heat and coolness include water, concrete, stone, brick, and tile. We incorporated these materials in a variety of ways in the houses of Village Homes. In the earliest homes, we stored water in tanks camouflaged as walls or culvert pipes sealed at both ends. Our later, more sophisticated designs used a solar greenhouse, a thick slab floor poured on top of rocks with pipes running through it, and a computer. The computer senses the temperature in the greenhouse and pulls warm air through the pipes in the floor during winter months. In summer, it pulls cool night air through the system.

To use solar energy effectively, one must take advantage of the position of the sun. In summer, the sun is high in the sky and traverses an arc of 240 degrees from east to west. In winter, the sun is low and traverses an arc of only 120 degrees from east to west. Proper orientation allows a home to maximize heat gain in winter and minimize unwanted heat gain in summer. A house that is longer from east to west and shorter from north to south, with most windows and a modest overhang on the south, can receive full sun in winter yet be fully shaded in summer. The shading comes from overhangs that are calculated to allow sunlight to come in during winter, when the sun is low, and to block sunlight in summer, when the sun is high. We also use arbors covered with deciduous vines. If springtime weather is cool, leafing on the arbors is delayed, allowing the house to stay warm, whereas a warm fall will keep leaves on the vines, providing needed shade. Solar greenhouses have sunscreens and are ventilated during summer.

To facilitate proper solar orientation of the homes, every lot in Village Homes is oriented north–south. The orientation of streets is essentially east–west. Because the streets curve slightly, lot shapes were varied to keep the north–south axis. This attention to solar orientation was innovative when Village Homes was constructed. Indeed, during construction, this feature proved unacceptable to the Federal Housing Administration (FHA), which refused loans for houses that were not perpendicular to the streets. We decided that energy-efficient housing was more important than availability of FHA loans and financed all the housing conventionally.

In Village Homes, overhangs are designed for solar access in winter and shading in summer.

With properly oriented houses, good insulation, a majority of south-facing windows shaded in summer with carefully calculated overhangs, many high-mass materials, and good ventilation, our home utility bills have been reduced by almost 50 percent.[3]

Almost every roof in Village Homes sports a solar water heater, making the houses fully self-sufficient with regard to water heating for seven months of every year. During the remaining months, solar energy provides 40 to 50 percent of water heating. The solar water-heating systems are installed along with reasonable water conservation devices. These include such inexpensive and readily available equipment as constrictors on shower heads and faucets, pressure reducers, aerators, better pipe insulation, and other measures. Strict application of all such measures can reduce hot water consumption to 20 to 25 percent of existing use.

The choice and placement of trees in Village Homes also facilitates solar access. Deciduous trees, predominantly Chinese tallows, were selected for street planting. They provide shade in summer but admit sunlight in winter. Taller trees and trees with massive branches were avoided because most of the homes have solar features on the roof and are positioned to take advantage of winter sun. Because solar energy is of utmost importance in Village Homes, the Declaration of Covenants, Conditions, and Restrictions signed by all homeowners prohibits residents from fencing their yards on the green-belt side or interfering with a neighbor's solar rights. These rights are further protected by the Architectural Review Board. A homeowner is, however, allowed to infringe on his or her own solar rights.

WALKING AND BICYCLING

Both Village Homes and, to a lesser extent, the city of Davis have made an effort to promote walking and bicycling. It is reported that there are more bikes than people in the city and that 25 percent of all trips are made by bike. Village Homes bike paths tie into those of the city and the University of California, the city's major employer. This is a campus where cars are discouraged and bicycles are encouraged; thus, many Village Homes residents ride a bike to work.

Our dead-end streets and grid of bike paths make it quicker to walk or bicycle to the Village Homes commercial or recreational areas or to the day-care center than to drive a car, thus creating incentives for more environmentally benign forms of transportation. Driving consumes half of all the energy used in California, but the Village Homes bike paths and mixed-use plan are saving a good deal of gasoline and keeping residents healthier by encouraging them to integrate exercise into their daily lives.

A grid of bicycle paths leads directly to all destinations in Village Homes.

A Design Closer to Nature

A sense of community and energy conservation are the philosophical foundation of the high quality of life in Village Homes, but the nuts and bolts of the actual design features have created an atmosphere of a natural environment within an urban setting. Although most of the houses face a street, fences, stucco walls, and shrubs have been placed along the streets to form private courtyards between street and house. Our long, narrow cul-de-sac streets function more as alleys. This arrangement replaces the wasted front lawn found in the typical subdivision.

Rather than being oriented toward the street, houses look out on common areas made up of a combination of heavily vegetated private and shared land, which creates a sense of considerable open space. Some homes overlook orchards, gardens, or vineyards. Neighborhood design guidelines prohibit the use of fences in these areas, but hedges, trees, and shrubs give a feeling

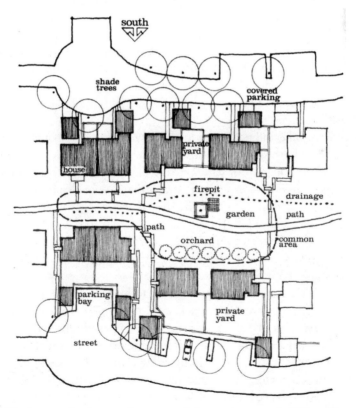

The house as it relates to the street and the common area in Village Homes.

Houses in Village Homes overlook common areas.

of privacy where it is desired. Although we feel as if we are living in a garden, in actual fact the houses in Village Homes are placed closer to the street and closer together than in most subdivisions. From inside the houses, automobile traffic is invisible.

Because the bike and pedestrian paths flow between the homes, the need for sidewalks on both sides of the streets was eliminated, thus narrowing the streets further. Installation of parking bays allowed us to decrease the width of the streets even more—by creating streets that do not also have to serve as parking lots, we were able to limit the paved area to that which is actually needed to provide parking for residents and their visitors. The typical width of a street in a suburban area is forty feet. In Village Homes, the streets range from twenty to twenty-six feet wide, and they could have been even narrower had the city allowed it.

Our small lots have encouraged people to build more compact houses, many of which are two-story homes. The cul-de-sac design also decreases the need to pave land. As a result of these features, 15 percent more land is available for other uses than is the case in the standard development in the city of Davis. Most of the liberated land in Village Homes has been used to create community orchards, vineyards, and vegetable gardens. These changes have also reduced the cost of the development by reducing infrastructure.

To conserve water, we have emphasized the use of drought-tolerant

Trees shade narrow streets in Village Homes.

plants and minimized the number of water-consuming plants. However, our primary emphasis has been on landscaping with plants that produce food.

NEIGHBORHOOD AGRICULTURE

In the construction phase, we surveyed thirty-six potential homeowners and asked them what proportion of their yards they would like to use for food production. Nineteen replied that they would like to use 10 to 40 percent, and twelve said they would like to use more than 40 percent. They viewed the incorporation of agricultural land and the availability of space for vegetable gardening as some of the most desirable features of the subdivision.

Responding to this interest, we dedicated seventeen acres of the land in Village Homes to agriculture; the eastern side of the community is bordered by a ring of 300 almond trees, and numerous smaller orchards are tucked between houses and along bike paths. Within the Village Homes development, almost every variety of food-producing fruit tree and shrub suitable for the climate is being grown on the common lands, including cherries, apricots, peaches, plums, pears, grapes, figs, persimmons, various citrus fruits, pomegranates, and almonds—as well as more exotic fruits such as jujubes and pineapple guavas. With the exception of the almonds, residents are invited to pick whatever they like without charge.

The edible landscape of Village Homes.

A Village Homes vineyard.

There is plenty of room in the common areas shared by clusters of eight homes to plant personal vegetable gardens, and many homeowners take advantage of that, growing primarily tomatoes, zucchini, basil, onions, melons, garlic, and eggplant during summer and spinach, broccoli, cauliflower, potatoes, and lettuce at other times of the year. Flowers are abundant too. Valued for the food they produce, fruit trees are more common than ornamentals in common areas. Many homes have a trellis over the south-facing windows that supports grapevines or kiwi fruit, providing shade during summer as well as tasty morsels to munch on.

In addition, seven acres of land on the western side of the development are available to residents for growing vegetables. These are well used by the serious gardeners, who want more garden space than that provided in their common areas. Two homeowners have actually made a business of this. One produces seedlings for nurseries, and the other was, for a time, growing vegetables that he harvested while young and sold to local restaurants. A vegetable garden in this area provides fresh produce for the Village Homes restaurant.

Because the crops are grown so close to the housing and play areas, pesticides are generally not used. Recently, however, the original insistence on organic gardening has been modified to allow a select few chemical fertilizers.

Row crops in Village Homes.

As mentioned earlier, the agricultural lands are overseen by the Agricultural Board, which makes decisions and recommendations regarding the agricultural component of Village Homes. Additionally, three paid gardeners, two of whom are residents, maintain the orchards, fields, greenbelts, and agricultural plantings. Their salaries are provided by the residents' monthly fees.

Originally, it was hoped that income from agricultural projects would someday offset a large portion of the gardening expenses. The almonds are currently grown as a cash crop; groups of residents pick them during the annual Village Homes almond harvest festival. However, the income from the almonds has offset only a small portion of the maintenance costs. In 1990, gardening and agricultural products provided an income of $5,200, as opposed to the $76,000 that went out in gardeners' salaries alone.

In determining the real financial effect of agriculture in Village Homes, several variables must be considered whose dollar value is hard to determine. The first variable is that maintenance of the agricultural land is comparable in cost to maintenance of the playing field, greenbelts, and ornamental areas, yet the agricultural areas also serve some of these same functions, providing a place for children to play and people to walk as well as visual open space.

The annual Village Homes almond harvest.

Maintenance costs in Village Homes compare favorably with those in condominium developments where the landscaping is entirely ornamental.

Moreover, the residents of Village Homes recover a certain portion of their monthly fees in fresh produce. We believe that if the greatest potential were realized, about 80 percent of the residents' fruit and vegetables could be grown within Village Homes. This portion would vary widely from family to family, but residents who maintain their own vegetable gardens in addition to harvesting the agricultural products grown in the community report that they purchase little or no additional produce. In Village Homes, we pick our food, carry it inside, and prepare it or eat it raw—and it is wonderfully fresh.

In Davis, where the replacement of prime farmland with housing subdivisions is an important and divisive topic, Village Homes presents a working alternative. Although the amount of food grown in Village Homes is not comparable to the amount previously grown on the same land when the acreage was completely given over to tomatoes, it is highly productive farmland. If the criterion used to assess the financial effect of agriculture is not simply amount but also variety, Village Homes compares favorably with the original farm.

Village Homes provides proof that it is possible to have the feeling of living in a rural setting at an overall residential density of four units per acre. There is a pastoral feeling about the neighborhood that provides residents with benefits beyond those of having plentiful, free, fresh food available year-round.

NATURAL DRAINAGE

Another feature that makes life in Village Homes seem closer to nature is the natural drainage system. The idea for the system was influenced by Michael's childhood experiences with water. In Seattle, Washington, where he lived when he was six years old, there was a creek near his house. It had water in it all year long, though only a trickle in the summer. It was his favorite place to play. He could watch the small trout or fish for them or just sit on the grassy bank and daydream. He picked morel mushrooms there in spring and blackberries in summer. When he was twenty, he went back to find that spot, but it was gone. The streambed had been filled and leveled and the water diverted into a concrete pipe under a street. It was sad to see that this precious place was not there for the next generation to enjoy. Thus, when it came time to design a neighborhood in which to live, one goal was to deal with runoff water as an asset for our own children to enjoy.

Cross section of a common area and drainage swale in Village Homes.

Whereas in the typical subdivision, lots are graded to slope toward the street so that water runs into the street and then into underground storm drains, which carry it away, in Village Homes we chose to do the opposite. Our lots are graded away from the street so that rainwater trickling off roofs and lawns finds its way into attractive, meandering, creeklike shallow swales that run through the common areas behind the houses. These swales carry the water slowly to larger channels that run through the greenbelts. They are landscaped like seasonal streambeds, with rocks, bushes, and trees. Runoff from streets goes directly into these larger channels. Small dams in the channels, just sturdy pieces of wood, help to slow the flow of water and prevent surges downstream. In light rains, this surface drainage system allows all the water that falls to be absorbed into the ground. In heavier rains, the system empties some water into the city's storm drains, but not nearly the amount

A conventional drainage system in a typical city of Davis neighborhood.

Natural drainage systems, such as the one at Village Homes, provide good places for children to play.

a typical subdivision would. Currently, we hold at least 90 percent of our runoff on-site. As our trees continue to make the soil more porous, the land's capacity to hold and absorb runoff increases.

The potential mosquito problem is easily managed. The creeks are designed either to drain completely within two or three days or to retain water year-round; the latter are stocked with mosquito fish, which happily feast on the mosquito larvae.

All of the surface drainage swales and channels in Village Homes were created artificially by grading because the natural drainage channels on the site had been obliterated years before, when the land was leveled for agricultural irrigation. Therefore, the new drainage channels conform to the street plan rather than vice versa. During excavation and grading of the site for streets and utilities, Michael found signs of a seasonal creek bed that had been filled in when the site was leveled for farming. It was, of course, too late to change the street plans, and we are not sure there would have been any advantage in restoring the channel in its original location, though we were able to create larger ponds in those areas so that the water would be more easily absorbed into the sand.

It is interesting to reflect that the natural drainage system of Village Homes was one of the most difficult innovations to get approved. Despite the fact that such a system seemed so serviceable, the city's Planning and

Year-round ponds in Village Homes are stocked with mosquito fish.

Water runs off a Village Homes street into a creeklike channel.

Ponds in Village Homes allow rainwater to be absorbed.

Building Department and Public Works Department were adamantly against it, and the FHA refused to approve it. Everyone said it would not work, that it would require continual maintenance and would not significantly reduce the amount of runoff. The planning director said that it would harbor vermin—an engineering term for wildlife, we assumed. So far, there have been no such problems. We have not experienced any disagreeable vermin, and the system has performed in a way that exceeded our expectations. It is extremely easy to maintain.

Allowing the soil to soak up rainwater has significantly reduced the amount of watering our plants require in spring and fall. But perhaps the nicest part of this system is the delightful sight of ponds and sound of water trickling through creeks during the rainy season. In his youth, our son, Christopher, spent many pleasurable hours with his friends playing in the shallow ponds and moving toy trucks through the mud. Another generation of children is now enjoying the same pastime.

Besides being an aesthetic amenity, a natural drainage system saves money for the developer. We saved about $800 per lot in 1975 dollars by avoiding construction of a storm sewer system. These savings paid the entire cost of landscaping the common areas.

Village Homes creek channels are attractive even without water in them.

Evaluation

Although most conservation features of the original Village Homes plan were implemented, the early plan also included an innovative feature that we failed to carry out: a sewage system that would have recycled treated sewage water to orchards and woodlots and gray water from showers and sinks to yards and shrubs. The county health department stopped us from carrying out this plan. However, after the construction of Village Homes was completed, new legislation was adopted in California that made explicit the authority of county health departments to approve gray-water systems.

Despite the incontrovertible economic success of Village Homes, it remains a unique accomplishment within our own community. The success of Village Homes did lead the city of Davis to reduce its street width requirements. Other subdivisions in the Davis area did adopt some solar features of Village Homes. A small federal grant funded a new energy ordinance in Davis, mandating the sort of lot and house orientation utilized in Village Homes. The ordinance also limited the glass area in homes and set out standards for insulation. These policies were eventually mandated through the state's energy conservation building code—adopted because of positive testimony provided by us and other solar builders in Davis.

Inspired by her experience with the city of Davis and Village Homes, Judy went on to found and direct a state commission called the Local Government Commission on Conservation and Renewable Energy Sources, which later became a nonprofit organization called the Local Government Commission. The philosophy of the commission, based in part on the Davis model, was that energy conservation is addressed most successfully at the local level rather than being mandated from above. The Local Government Commission brought together elected officials from different communities to share experience and expertise and build enthusiasm. A variety of local energy ordinances were passed within California as a result. However, with the exception of these solar strategies, the design and philosophies of Village Homes did not find immediate, widespread acceptance.

According to former city manager Howard Reese, the International City/County Management Association issued an evaluation of Village Homes according to two criteria: was it innovative, and was it transferable? The report gave Village Homes high marks in both areas, yet Reese said that the many managers who came to visit Village Homes and to talk to him concurred that similar subdivisions in their areas would be difficult to push through. Even twenty years later, despite a growing interest in natural drainage, solar energy, and dispersed agriculture, most of these features would be hard to get approved in most jurisdictions in the United States.

Village Homes itself has undergone some changes. Physically, the plantings have matured, making it a more beautiful place to live. The narrow streets have created none of the difficulties for emergency vehicles that city staff members originally feared they might. Residents who initially chafed at restrictions forbidding street parking and antennae on roofs no longer even notice them. Visitors to Village Homes may complain of not knowing where to park and of then not being able to find the front door, but residents value the scenery and the peace and quiet.

The solar features have worked effectively and unobtrusively. Additional solar greenhouses have been added to several houses.

The natural drainage system was tested during several years of twice the normal rainfall and found to work extremely well. Unlike the streets elsewhere in the city, streets in Village Homes have never flooded.

In Village Homes, the relocation of automobile traffic away from front doors has helped to create an exceptionally safe environment for small children. The orchards are in peak years of production. It is paradise for the children. They wander anywhere they want, snacking on fresh fruit picked from the orchards. Although many of the houses have been remodeled for larger families, outgrowing the house seems to be the primary reason a family leaves Village Homes but remains in the Davis area.

The makeup of the Village Homes population is changing, slowly and inevitably. The original plan explicitly sought residents from all economic backgrounds. The houses tended to be small and modest, and apartments and low-cost housing were included. Unfortunately, as Village Homes has increasingly come to be seen as a desirable place to live, more and more families have been priced out of it. However, there are still affordable apartments, some small houses with affordable price tags, and a co-op house available to lower-income individuals.

The level of involvement with the homeowners' association is less than it was initially, but perhaps this can be read as a positive indicator. If people were unhappy with their lives in Village Homes, they would be involved. If they become unhappy, the mechanism is in place to allow them to address the problems. The annual almond harvest festival and other homeowners' events are well attended, but most social events in Village Homes tend to be small in scale and spontaneous.

Village Homes is not an ordinary place to live. The landscaping and design of the subdivision continue to foster a close-knit neighborhood that is an increasingly rare phenomenon in modern society. The setting is unusually attractive. Elimination of the need for air conditioners by means of our natural cooling system creates a quieter neighborhood and allows us to be more in touch with the natural breezes and smells of summer. We dine on the freshest fruits and vegetables year-round, and when it rains, we enjoy the sound of raindrops in the creeks and ponds.

Yet the biggest success of Village Homes is arguably its day-to-day ordinariness. Village Homes provides evidence that it is possible to live in a beautiful, natural setting, to live in greater harmony with the environment, and to live as part of a community—to live, in fact, in a very ordinary, comfortable, and enjoyable way.

Its perceived ordinariness is a plus if Village Homes is to inspire more sustainable development on a large scale. We have not given up hope of realizing this goal. Civano in Tucson, Arizona, labeled a grandchild of Village Homes on a much larger scale, is now under construction. Other sustainable new development projects, either proposed or under construction, include Prairie Crossing near Chicago, Illinois; Haymount in Virginia; Coffee Creek Center in northern Indiana; and Dewees Island, a vacation retreat in South Carolina built according to the principles of sustainable development. For the first time, we are being asked to speak at seminars held by organizations representing mainstream builders and developers. Recently, Village Homes was presented as a model for new development in publications issued by both the National Association of Home Builders and the Natural Resources Defense Council. Something new is definitely in the air!

Chapter 3

The Basis for Sustainable Development

The design of Village Homes evolved from a number of commonly held scientific and psychological assumptions that we believe provide the basis for sustainable urban design. From these assumptions, we developed the goals that guided our design. This chapter may seem theoretical to some readers. However, if one takes the time to consider these assumptions, the concepts presented in this book—including that of garden cities and garden villages—will be more meaningful.

Assumptions

Of the eight assumptions presented here, the first four are based on ecological principles. They also reflect, in a subtle way, a general view of humanity's relationship to the earth, a relationship embodied in a number of centuries-old philosophies—intuitive wisdom that is now being borne out by science. This relationship is expressed well in a Native American proverb, "We must all see ourselves as part of this earth, not as an enemy from the outside who tries to impose his will on it. We who know the meaning of the pipe also know that, being a living part of the earth, we cannot harm any part of her without hurting ourselves."[1] The last four assumptions deal more with the effect of the human-made environment on people. In considering all these assumptions, readers should keep in mind that they are intended to link urban design with current ecological and social problems.

1. Every living thing survives by numerous and subtle relationships with all living things and with the inanimate environment.

When all living things are considered together, the relationships among them appear as complex, interdependent, and self-regulating structures or ecosystems in which any one form of life depends on the rest of the system to provide the conditions necessary for its existence. Human beings are as much a part of this ecosystem as is any other form of life and depend on the rest of the ecosystem for food, a breathable atmosphere, drinkable water, and a survivable climate. The earth has not always provided a suitable environment for humans but was made hospitable over the millennia by a functioning ecosystem.[2] Changes in the ecosystem could eventually reverse the process that made our planet livable.

Human technology permits powerful manipulations of the various elements of the ecosystem. Changes intended to improve human life and comfort by satisfying needs and desires often have side effects that alter or destroy parts of the ecosystem. For example, human manipulation of the ecosystem has, within a few lifetimes, destroyed vast amounts of farmland and killed the fish in hundreds of lakes. Scientists increasingly warn us of larger-scale changes, already under way, that will have devastating effects on all life. A case in point is the burning of fossil fuels, which is releasing huge amounts of carbon dioxide into the atmosphere at the same time that other pollutants are gradually migrating to the upper atmosphere and reducing the concentration of ozone there. The changes in carbon dioxide and ozone levels are altering the way the atmosphere transmits, reflects, absorbs, and reradiates the sun's energy.

Scientists warn that global warming has crossed the line from theory to documented reality. This raises the alarming possibility that in the future, melting polar ice caps will significantly raise the sea level, flooding seaboard cities and inundating vast areas of fertile land. Dramatic temperature shifts also threaten to make much of our food-producing land either unproductive or much less productive.

Ozone depletion is allowing more ultraviolet light to reach the earth. This in turn is increasing the rate of skin cancer. It is also reducing seed germination. It could eventually destroy much of the ocean's plankton—microscopic plants that produce 70 percent of our oxygen supply. Combined with continued deforestation through human activity, this will lead to a gradual decrease in the amount of oxygen in the atmosphere, subjecting us and other animals to a type of stress now experienced only at very high altitudes. These are just the more obvious of the critical problems that need to be addressed through better urban design and land use planning.

2. *Ecosystems and parts of ecosystems composed of a wide variety of species tend to adapt better to environmental changes or human tampering than do those composed of fewer species.*

According to Ashby's law of the requisite variety in cybernetic systems, a system formed by more elements with greater diversity is less subject to fluctuations than is a less diverse system.[3] This is an argument for maintaining a wide variety of crop and livestock species and diverse agricultural systems. For example, potato blight caused devastating famine in Ireland in 1845–1849 partly because of the inhabitants' widespread reliance on that single crop.

It appears that a similar principle applies to human communities. Those communities with the greatest diversity in energy sources, forms of economic enterprise, and food sources will tend to be more stable and adapt most successfully and painlessly to changes, be they environmental, political, economic, or social. Sustainable urban design, then, would require a reversal of current toward less diverse environments.

3. Part of the ecosystem is a complex system of energy transfers that depends, ultimately, on energy input.

Until relatively recent times, the sun provided the only significant energy input, and consequently the ecosystem is best adapted to this source of energy. Nuclear fuels and natural fossil fuels introduce significant energy inputs to which the ecosystem is not adapted, and they yield by-products that change the chemical balance and radiation levels in the environment.

Increased radiation from the nuclear industry can cause cancer, leukemia, and damaging genetic changes. Burning of fossil fuels is contributing to a rise in the earth's temperature through the greenhouse effect. Acid rain, a result of gases produced by burning coal, can damage or kill agricultural crops and natural vegetation and has killed fish in many lakes and rivers. Air pollution, also created by the burning of fossil fuels, can damage human health and mental capacity. Urban design must be modified so that it can operate on renewable energy forms that do not negatively affect the environment's ability to sustain human life.

4. In the long run, every one of humanity's physical needs must be satisfied either without the use of nonrenewable resources or through recovery and reuse of those resources.

Lumber is an example of a renewable resource when it is consumed no more rapidly than it is generated by the ecosystem. Nonrenewable resources such as metals, which are not generated by the ecosystem, or petroleum products, which are generated so slowly as to be classified as nonrenewable, need to be recovered and recycled, or, alternatively, their use needs to be avoided altogether.

There is a danger inherent in planning and building systems that depend on using a renewable resource faster than it is generated or using a nonrenewable resource without recycling it. Such use cannot be sustained. In addition, our current dependence on a single energy source (fossil fuels) allows us to specialize in the use of that resource instead of meeting our needs in diverse ways. Lacking diversity, we are more likely to find ourselves in serious trouble (according to assumption 2) when the inevitable shortages occur.

This is precisely the current situation. Fossil fuels are nonrenewable resources, and we have depended on them so heavily for our energy needs that as they become scarcer, we face a difficult transition to renewable energy sources such as solar, wind, hydroelectric, and geothermal power and biomass conversion. Most of us cannot even imagine making this transition. Had we relied partly on these other energy sources all along, it would be much simpler to imagine and to carry out such a transition now. Ecological design will accomplish this task.

5. *Although humans seem to be the most adaptable of living things, we still have certain inherent physical and psychological needs that must be met by the ecosystem, the human-made physical environment, and the social environment.*
Psychologist and philosopher Abraham Maslow proposed that basic human needs can be arranged in a hierarchy according to their urgency. He rated physiological needs such as those for food, water, and warmth as most urgent, followed by the needs for security, social interaction, esteem, and realization of one's human potential, in that order. All of these needs, however, are real and important. Providing for an individual's more urgent needs allows him or her to devote attention to less urgent needs and thus reach higher levels of satisfaction and fulfillment of human potential—or, to use Maslow's term, self-actualization.[4]

It follows from this that some environments potentially allow their inhabitants to reach higher levels of fulfillment and well-being than do other environments. Urban planners and others who design living environments must be aware of our responsibilities to optimize that potential. In doing so, we must give as much attention to the factors that influence the social environment as to the physical systems. For example, we should not optimize the design of streets and street patterns for automobile and fire engine use but ignore their effect on social interaction.

6. *Humans are for the most part genetically adapted to the environment that existed from about 200 to 20,000 years ago. This adaptation involves not*

just our physical makeup but also our modes of perception and behavior and relates to the social environment as well as the physical environment.

As a species, humans are genetically better equipped to live and thrive in some social settings than in others, just as we are better equipped for some physical environments than for others. The human race may not be genetically adapted to mass society or to the social effects of a high-technology lifestyle or a chaotic visual environment.

René Dubos stated:

> Social contacts may have been more satisfying by the fire in a Stone Age cave or on a village bench than they are now through the convenience of telephone conversations and of other means of mass communication. Dancing to the sound of drums in the savanna or to a fiddler on the village green could be as exciting as dancing to electronic music. Throwing a rock at an enemy was a more satisfying way to express anger or hatred than killing him at long range with a gun or a bomb. The fundamental satisfactions and passions of humankind are thus still much as they were before the advent of the automobile, of the airplane, and of the television set; before the era of steam and electric power; and even before our ancestors had abandoned hunting for agriculture and for industry and had moved from the cave to the village or the city. In many cases, furthermore, modern life has rather impoverished the methods by which fundamental urges can be expressed. Modern societies can escape from boredom only by direct sensory experiences of primitive life; the need for these experiences persists in the modern world for the simple reason that it is indelibly inscribed in the genetic code of the human species.[5]

This suggests that village life or "tribal" life in groups of fifty to a few thousand persons in a natural setting may provide the most hospitable environment for human life.

Typical modern environments are much more stressful. We personally believe that confrontation with the automobile may be a serious source of this stress. This does not mean that the automobile does not have a place in the urban environment. It offers a convenient form of transportation that is often pleasurable. The problem is the way that roads now dominate urban design.

The list of ways in which automobiles generate stress is a long one. Their noise and exhaust fumes and the visual and tactile harshness of both automobiles and roadways affect both drivers and pedestrians. Streets and parking areas form barriers to pedestrian traffic and create obstacle courses in both commercial and residential areas, demanding that pedestrians be constantly alert for moving vehicles and parents pay constant attention to their children's safety. Thirty-nine percent of all deaths among children aged twelve and younger occur when the children are hit by a car while walking or riding bicycles.[6]

Automobiles stress people in even more ways. They isolate us from all but visual contact with our surroundings and carry us through the surroundings so rapidly that even visual impressions are vague and superficial and chances for social contact are nil. Automobile use deprives us of the healthy and invigorating mild exercise we could get by walking. Health professionals now consider lack of exercise and poor diet a health threat secondary only to cigarette smoking.[7]

7. The relationship between people and the environment goes both ways: humanity both shapes and is shaped by its environment.

It is critical that we realize our interrelationship with our environment if we are to break away from social patterns that are detrimental to our well-being. Take the example of a typical suburban neighborhood. Because we are a society of mobile individuals with only weak community ties, we design our new neighborhoods with more concern for mobility than for community life. These neighborhoods frustrate whatever inclination toward community we still have and keep us from learning how to get along with one another. Author and social critic Murray Bookchin describes this process well:

> Historically, the basis for a vital urban entity consisted not primarily of its design elements but of the nuclear relations between people that produced these elements. Human scale was more than a design on a drawing board; it emerged from the intimate association provided by the clan, the guild, and the civic union of free, independent farmers and craftsmen. Knitted together at the base of a civic entity, people created a city that formally and structurally sheltered their most essential and meaningful social relations. If these relations were balanced and harmonious, so too were the design elements of the city. If, on the other hand, they were distorted and antagonistic, the design elements of the city revealed this in its monumentalism and extravagant growth. Hierarchical social relations produced hierarchical space; egalitarian relations, egalitarian space. Until city planning addresses itself to the need for a radical critique of the prevailing transformation of existing social relations, it will remain mere ideology—the servant of the very society that is producing the urban crises of our time.[8]

Individuals who have not experienced life in a true community may not be aware of its value. Yet a sustainable environment must allow people to achieve an optimum quality of life by supporting human social needs.

8. Humans can adapt to a wide range of environmental conditions, but the result of adaptation to inhospitable conditions is temporary or chronic stress.
Victims of stress created by inhospitable conditions can reduce that stress by becoming insensitive to the stimuli that cause it, but this produces a general deadening—a lack of awareness and responsiveness—that is equally harmful. Stress in its various forms and insensitivity in response to stress contribute to a wide variety of human afflictions: heart disease, mental illness, and a general lowering of resistance to disease; destructive use of drugs and alcohol; apathy and cynicism; crime; and a loss of sensitivity and compassion, to name only a few.

Our daily exposure to the unnatural stimulation of the modern environment is a constant burden on our capacity to function well. It wears down each individual differently. Imagine ocean waves constantly pounding against a cliff. Sooner or later, the waves will break down the cliff; the length of time this takes depends on the strength of the particular formation. Long before the formation falls, however, there is erosion.

To understand what causes stress and to avoid designing it into our environment is a responsibility that cannot be ignored as it has been in the past. Stress caused by noise provides a good example.

Research has shown noise to be a contributory or aggravating factor in human disease. Noise has been implicated in such disorders as loss of hearing, hypertension, ulcers and other gastric malfunction, migraine headaches, insomnia, colitis, and mental illness.[9] But perhaps of greatest concern is the effect of noise on the cardiovascular system. It has been well documented that exposure to noise (both loud, sudden noise and lower-level, continuous noise such as city traffic noise) can cause such reactions as vasoconstriction, raised blood cholesterol levels, high blood pressure, and irregular heartbeat.[10] Moreover, although noise has not been proven to be a direct cause of death due to heart attack, it is well established that the risk of heart attack is higher when one or more of the previously mentioned symptoms of noise exposure is present. Therefore, a connection between noise and risk of heart attack may be inferred. Indeed, the evidence was adequate to convince former U.S. surgeon general William H. Stewart, who made the following statement in a keynote address to the nation's first conference on noise as a health hazard:

> Donora [noise-induced] incidents occur daily in communities
> across the U.S. Not in terms of specific numbers of deaths attrib-
> utable to excessive noise exposure, but in terms of many more
> than 20 cardiovascular problems for which the noises of twenti-
> eth-century living are a major contributory factor.[11]

Even the noises we think we are used to cannot be considered anything less than sources of constant irritation. Furnaces, refrigerators, air conditioners, and the neighbors' radios, television sets, and phonographs all prevent us from experiencing the peace and quiet we occasionally need for real physical and mental health.

We manage to ignore these stimuli as we do all unavoidable irritating stimuli. But when we shut out a stressful stimulus, we are also likely to reduce our sensitivity to other stimuli coming through the same sensory channel. Wilderness campers often notice that their hearing becomes keener after a day or two away from civilization, suggesting that in the city their hearing had become less sensitive in order to shut out the stressful noise.

Visual incongruity most likely has a similar effect. It may be more subtle, but it nevertheless reduces our sensitivity to visual beauty.

From the eight assumptions presented here, a statement of goals or design principles can be extracted. We personally believe that the Ahwahnee Principles, detailed earlier, serve as a comprehensive set of design guidelines that successfully integrate these assumptions about humans and the environment.

With goals that are complete and well defined, there is a much better chance of producing a good solution. However, a good solution also depends on the process used in planning, both in selecting goals and in creating plans and designs that are true to those goals. Chapters 4, 5, and 6 examine the basic needs and related goals that must be addressed in planning sustainable communities; chapter 7 details the broader aspects that must be considered when locating human settlements; and chapters 8 and 9 lay out an urban design and a design process that integrate environmental, social, and economic goals.

Chapter 4

Water, Food, Shelter: The Basics

As a society, it is important to consider how we will satisfy our basic needs as we prepare for the design of our communities, towns, and regions— both when designing new development and when renewing existing cities. How can we ensure that we will have a substantial supply of safe water and food? How can we best provide adequate housing for our entire population? How can we be sure we will have the resources we need to sustain ourselves and our grandchildren into the future, and how can we use these resources efficiently? In answering these questions, this chapter addresses the basic needs of water and food, as well as housing for lower-income families. Also suggested are public policies and individual actions supportive of changes that are inevitable if society is to sustain itself. They are included in this book because they will be an integral part of a sustainable society.

A community that meets most of its basic needs locally and regionally is more stable—from both an environmental and an economic perspective. A community that cannot do so is more subject to hardships caused by economic disruptions, unforeseen natural catastrophes, and global shortages in resources. A community that is able to meet its own basic needs is also more economically efficient because it uses less energy than does a community that must import a high percentage of its food or transport water for long distances.

This book is not advocating total self-sufficiency or the economic insularity that existed in communities before the advent of the railroad and highway. It merely presents the argument that there is no need to organize our economy so that all the things we need to survive must be shipped in, using large amounts of energy and resources, as is the case in too many communities today.

Water: Supply, Quality, and Flood Control

In the hierarchy of physical priorities for human existence, the need for water ranks above the needs for food, clothing, and shelter. Second only to air as a necessity for survival, water plays a role in every aspect of our lives. Our bodies are about 65 percent water by weight. For plants, the percentage can be much higher.

We are inextricably bound up with the cycling and recycling of water through the ecosystem. The same water we carry today as body weight may have come fairly recently from the sea. Having evaporated from and subsequently returned to the earth as rain or snow, it was drawn from rivers or from wells, and we absorbed it by drinking and eating. After leaving our bodies, this same water will return to the atmosphere, eventually to rain down again over land or sea; the cycle continues without end. Because we are a part of this cycle, our well-being depends on the purity and reliability of our water system.

Although each of us needs a regular supply of drinking water to sustain ourselves, that amount is small compared with what we use every day around the house and the amount we use in agriculture and industry. A gallon of water per day meets our needs for drinking water, but according to a 1989 study using statistics gathered by the California Department of Water Resources and the U.S. Department of Agriculture, 365 gallons of water are required to grow a dollar's worth of grapes, 1,818 gallons for a dollar's worth of rice, and 12,500 gallons for a dollar's worth of pasture, most of which is used for beef or milk production.[1]

Because water is essential to human life and the functioning of society, people have always tended to settle mostly in areas with good natural water supplies. Before the development of modern well-drilling technology, the location of communities was more limited to areas with sufficient surface-water resources or shallower aquifers. More recently, technological development and cheap fossil-fuel energy have allowed water to be brought in from deep underground aquifers or from areas with abundant water. Dams, aqueducts, deep wells, and advanced water purification systems have allowed many cities to expand in areas of scant rainfall and very limited local surface-water or groundwater supplies.

Today, however, many of the technological breakthroughs of the past are proving to be inadequate and people are drinking water that is harmful to their health. A report by the Environmental Working Group and the Natural Resources Defense Council states:

More than 45 million Americans in thousands of communities were served drinking water during 1994–1995 that was polluted with fecal matter, parasites, disease causing microbes, radiation, pesticides, toxic chemicals, and lead at levels that violated health standards established under the federal Safe Drinking Water Act. More than 18,500 public water supplies reported at least one violation of a federal drinking water health standard during this two year period.[2]

At the same time, our efforts to increase water supply are having unintended consequences. As a result of the construction of dams and development on floodplains and in wetlands, more than sixty freshwater-dependent aquatic species are facing extinction in central and northern California alone. Under the Endangered Species Act as it is presently written, these species must be protected even if it means dramatic changes in current methods of operating dams and water projects.[3]

One of the least talked-about problems with dams is the ultimate cost of decommissioning them when their useful and safe lives are over. Huge quantities of silt, often polluted with mining wastes such as mercury, have to be removed, and the dams themselves must be taken down to prevent catastrophic events as they get older, more fragile, and more likely to break in a major flood event or an earthquake. Currently, water suppliers fail to incorporate this cost in their water-pricing systems.

Today, the political will is almost gone for the large state and federal appropriations that have financed dam building for almost 100 years. The antitax and deficit reduction crusade has combined with the widely supported environmental movement to make it almost impossible to authorize and appropriate funds for new dams. With the old solutions not politically or financially possible, new solutions must be found.

Another problem is that groundwater supplies are being threatened with overdrafting such that they cannot even keep up with today's level of consumption, much less the increased demand expected in the future. To make matters worse, groundwater is continually being contaminated, and it is becoming increasingly difficult to purify the water adequately to meet federal and state drinking-water standards. In agricultural areas, a major source of contamination is the pesticides, fertilizers, fumigants, and other chemicals used on crops. However, even groundwater in urban areas is likely to be contaminated by the fertilizers and herbicides applied to lawns and gardens. In some areas, chemical application rates for yards, parks, and especially golf courses are actually higher than in agricultural fields.

Gas station holding tanks, automobile repair shops, manufacturers, weapons developers, and other business enterprises also threaten to contaminate groundwater supplies with trichloroethylene (TCE), methyl tertiary butyl ether (MTBE), polychlorinated biphenyls (PCBs), dioxins, and hundreds of other chemicals. New methods are being developed to pump water from the ground and clean it as a way of stopping contaminated plumes from spreading to and shutting down drinking-water wells, but some chemicals are defying scientists' best efforts to neutralize them. Where purification does work, the costs are high, and pressure is mounting to find cheaper alternatives.

Scientists say that this is very likely only the tip of the pyramid of groundwater contamination because of the length of time it takes for contaminants to leach down to well depths. The first plumes created by the use of chemicals in the 1950s and 1960s are just now showing up in drinking-water wells. In many areas, contamination created by increased use in the 1970s and 1980s and the increased number of locations of use will not become obvious for another decade. Maintenance of groundwater aquifers as sustainable sources of drinking water will take ever-increasing financial and technical investment.

Growing populations will exacerbate problems with water supply and quality as more demand is placed on diminishing supplies. We are most acutely aware of this during prolonged dry periods. Droughts tend to reveal the overextension of our water systems and increase the already enormous costs inflicted on fish, wildlife, wetlands, and water-dependent habitat. Scientists predict that global warming will increase the extremes in our weather patterns. Thus, we can expect longer and more pronounced droughts.

Global warming is also predicted to result in an increased number of storm, tornado, hurricane, and flood catastrophes. The Federal Emergency Management Agency reported that since the 1940s, flood damage has increased in terms of both dollars and lost human lives, in spite of the agency's increasing investment in flood control projects. The problem is exacerbated by the fact that local governments are allowing development on floodplains under the assumption that the economic benefits of developing on "100-year" floodplains outweigh the long-term costs. The term *100-year flood* means that in any year, there is a 1 percent chance that a flood event will occur. But as time has passed, it has become increasingly evident that planners have underestimated the frequency of such floods.[4] The director of the Milwaukee Metropolitan Sewerage District, for instance, told us in 1998 that 100-year floods had occurred in the district's jurisdiction for the past two years in a row. Personnel of the agency no longer believe that these floods are a once-in-a-lifetime occurrence in their region.

There is one final area of concern regarding water supply in many parts of the country. The infrastructure that carries water is decaying. Everything built by people—such as wells, canals, levees, pipes, and sewage treatment plants—will need to be replaced in the future. The baby boom generation will have to make huge investments of labor and capital to reconstruct and rebuild a significant portion of the water infrastructure.

The solution to these problems lies in creating an infrastructure and a system for distributing water that will be sustainable over the long term. This will require that communities work harmoniously with nature, creating an infrastructure that works synergistically, not just as a set of single-purpose functions. This means focusing simultaneously on water conservation and pollution prevention, developing more sustainable water supplies, devising more effective flood control strategies, and halting construction on floodplains. It means choosing water supply and flood control strategies that preserve endangered species, and it means recycling and reusing our precious water supplies.

A number of ongoing efforts initiated by nonprofit groups, local governments, and developers represent steps in the right direction. The following are but a few examples.

The water supply problems in the Los Angeles Basin are enormous. Officials of the Metropolitan Water District of Southern California (MWD) envision that the agency will need to import at least 50,000 additional acre-feet of water each year if the region's population increases at the rates currently projected.[5] But TreePeople, one of the oldest and largest environmental organizations in Los Angeles, has been developing and demonstrating cost-effective alternatives that can simultaneously address concerns about flood control, water supply, and water quality along with other serious environmental challenges. Among these alternatives are cisterns that catch, filter, and store rainwater from rooftop gutters for use in landscape irrigation during dry months. The TreePeople approach combines the cisterns with tree planting, mulching, and water retention techniques in a multibenefit approach. TreePeople estimates that if most water users in Los Angeles combined the use of cisterns with other recommended conservation practices, the city could reduce its dependence on imported water by as much as 50 percent. The cisterns are also designed to serve as flood control devices. They can be slowly drained prior to a major storm event, increasing their storage capacity.[6]

In the city of Davis, treated sewage water is delivered to a 400-acre wetland. In addition to serving as a means of flood control, a water purification system, and a mechanism for replenishing groundwater, the wetland provides excellent habitat for wildlife and waterfowl traveling the Pacific Flyway.

Other communities recycle water that would otherwise be sent to sewage plants. A California law passed in the early 1990s allows local public health departments to approve the diversion of gray water for such uses. (Gray water is water that drains from drinking fountains, sinks, and the like.) Some communities have dual water-piping systems so that gray water is piped to ornamental fountains and sewage water is piped to a sewage treatment plant. Others deliver gray water or partially treated sewage water to golf courses and parks. This not only saves water but also reduces the cost of treating the water. In California, 250 water recycling systems are in operation, with another 165 scheduled to come on-line.[7]

Some local governments require that builders install low-flow showerheads and low-flush toilets in new construction. Others also encourage retrofitting of existing homes with these devices. The MWD is saving more than 50,000 acre-feet of water per year with the 1.5 million low-flush toilets it has paid to be retrofitted. By 2003, the agency plans to almost double the number of 1.5-gallon toilets installed and the amount of water saved. At $500 per acre-foot, by 2003, MWD customers will be saving more than $50 million per year.[8]

Another important strategy for reducing water consumption is the use of drought-tolerant species or native plant species. In areas where rainfall is not enough to keep lawns green, lawns should be used sparingly.

Berkeley, California, among other cities, is turning to integrated pest management. This technique for controlling pests avoids the use of chemical pesticides and prevents water pollution by using more natural, time-tested means of controlling pests.

Reducing pavement also has a positive effect on water quality. According to the Environmental Protection Agency, runoff or nonpoint-source pollution accounts for about 60 percent of all surface-water pollution in the United States. A compact development pattern can reduce runoff by two-thirds of that generated by sprawl development.[9]

In Village Homes, we have addressed the issues of water conservation, flood control, and groundwater protection with strategies that work in an integrated manner. These strategies include compact development with narrow streets, a natural drainage system, use of organic gardening methods, and use of drought-tolerant plants, with large expanses of lawn used only where needed for sports activities. Each individual strategy has multiple benefits.

The homeowners' association regulates the use of pesticides in common areas and greenbelts in order to protect groundwater supplies and human health. This restraint in use of toxic chemicals is made possible in part by our avoidance of monocultures—large areas planted with only one species. The mixture of trees, shrubs, and numerous varieties of food-producing plants has created an ecosystem that is more diverse and therefore more disease resistant. The number of species of birds found in the community, for instance, seems to grow every year.

There are a number of new conservation technologies that we would install if we were building today. In the future, we will need to retrofit our homes with low-flow showerheads and low-flush toilets. We did attempt to use a dual plumbing system in some of the homes to divert gray water into the landscape. However, as mentioned in chapter 2, this was almost fifteen years before the state of California made it clear that local public health departments have the authority to permit such systems.

The design details of any community's water system will depend on the unique characteristics of the local environment and the resources available. Whatever type of system is adopted, it should meet some basic requirements: efficient use of energy; high-quality, effective flood control; species preservation; and long-term sustainability without contamination. To the degree that water systems pass these tests, society will be on its way to sound management of this essential resource.

In the final analysis, conserving water supplies, keeping them pure, and using them wisely will require each community to act on its own behalf. Communities will have to do this in the context of regional planning so that growth in each region is limited in accordance with the amount of water that is available on a sustainable basis. Author Richard J. Barnet states, "The most persuasive students of water politics seem to be those who urge the return to local communities of the responsibility for providing a safe and ample water supply."[10]

Food Production

Food is next on the list of basic human needs. Because of the quantity we eat and because we must eat on a regular basis, food gathering and production has been one of the major activities of humans from the early hunter-gatherers to today's farmers, food processors, and grocery shoppers.

Of all the changes humanity has undergone, the adoption of cultivation techniques, which brought about changes in the way we secure our food supplies, may be the most significant. It allowed people for the first time to augment the production of the natural environment and to settle down and form the first permanent communities. As agricultural techniques were improved, largely through the use of plows and draft animals, production efficiency increased, enabling larger and larger concentrations of people to live far from their source of food.

Today, only the smallest fraction of the food consumed in the average town in the United States is produced in or around the town. The rest is shipped in, often from great distances. There is no inherent reason, other than climatic constraints, why this must be so. Today's towns have to import virtually all the food their residents need for survival, primarily because the towns were planned with no thought for food production.

This situation exists because over the years, we have changed from a system of local production and consumption to a system of highly specialized, centralized production and distribution for consumption all over the country, indeed, the world. Thus, today few workers in the United States are involved in farming. Almost all basic food needs are met by large-scale, highly mechanized agriculture that is dependent on fossil fuels and chemical fertilizers and pesticides.

In addition to reducing community self-sufficiency, modern industrialized agriculture has brought with it many social and environmental problems. Most of these problems are summed up in a 1980 report on organic farming published by the U.S. Department of Agriculture. In reference to a survey, the report states:

> It has been most apparent in conducting this study that there is increasing concern about the adverse effects of our U.S. agricultural production system, particularly in regard to the intensive and continuous production of cash grains and the extensive and sometimes excessive use of agricultural chemicals. Among the concerns most often expressed are:
>
> (1) Sharply increasing costs and uncertain availability of energy and chemical fertilizers and our heavy reliance on these inputs.
> (2) Steady decline in soil productivity and tilth from excessive soil erosion and loss of soil organic matter.
> (3) Degradation of the environment from erosion and sedimentation, and from pollution of natural waters by agricultural chemicals.

(4) Hazards to human and animal health and to food safety from heavy use of pesticides.

(5) Demise of the family farm and localized marketing systems.[11]

Large-scale mechanized food production requires considerable amounts of energy. In fact, of all the energy consumed in the United States, 9 percent goes to food production. Large farm equipment used in planting and harvesting literally gobbles up fossil fuels, and still more energy is burned in transporting, refrigerating, and packaging the foods.

Current farming methods threaten the aquifer supplies in almost every part of the country, both by consuming more water than is replenished each year and by contaminating the water. For example, in 1994, California's agricultural businesses used 28 million acre-feet of water, compared with the 6.6 million acre-feet consumed for residential use.[12] At the same time, pesticides, fertilizers, fumigants, and other chemicals leach into the groundwater and over time contaminate water farther beneath the surface. Some of these chemicals do not break down into neutral by-products over time and find their way into drinking-water wells. Tests conducted by the California State Department of Health Services showed that well more than half of the

Neighborhood-scale agriculture in Village Homes avoids the use of pesticides and saves the energy otherwise needed for farming equipment, transportation, and packaging.

groundwater wells in San Joaquin County are contaminated with the agricultural chemical DBCP (1,2-dibromo-3-chloropropane).[13] Residents in many rural homes must drink bottled water but still risk the health effects of these chemicals when they shower.

Many geologists and soil chemists predict that eventually, all wells in agricultural areas will have unacceptable levels of contamination by farm chemicals. Depending on the soils, current and historical levels of application, and the types of chemicals used, the pollutants will migrate downward and reach the wells' intake level. In Davis, for example, all shallow (100-foot) wells are being closed because nitrates from fertilizer application are migrating horizontally from nearby agricultural fields into the aquifer beneath the city. An unknown question is whether these pollutants will reach the new 500-foot wells and, if so, how long it will take for them to do so.

A final drawback of large-scale mechanized food production that one cannot really put a price on but that is real nonetheless is the deteriorating quality of food. Today's tomatoes, for instance, are bred not for taste but for ease in mechanical harvesting and convenience in packing.

To begin to solve all these problems, we will have to take three steps. The first is to move in the direction of ecologically sound farming. Quoting again from the Department of Agriculture's report on organic farming:

> Much can be learned from organic farming about reducing soil erosion and nonpoint source pollution. Small farms, many of the mixed crop/livestock farms, and farms with access to ample quantities of organic wastes, could be shifted to organic farming methods in the future without having a large impact on total agricultural production.[14]

Fortunately, ecologically sound farming methods are becoming more widely accepted. In Yolo County, California, the Yolo County Resource Conservation District has been helping farmers teach their neighbors new techniques to help save money over the long term, recharge groundwater, produce cleaner effluent, and provide wildlife habitat. The county now has more than 500 on-farm ponds that hold irrigation runoff before it is pumped back to the fields. Once the infrastructure is in place, it is often cheaper and more energy efficient to pump water from the pond than from the ground. Most agricultural chemicals in irrigation return-water become less toxic over time, and certain plants in the ponds, such as cattails, further purify the water. Water held in the pond does not run off and pollute the nearest stream or river. Rain fills the pond and less rainfall runs off, resulting in more water being absorbed into the ground and less water joining a flood event downstream. On-farm ponds act as did the wetlands that were on the land before it was first plowed and planted.

New irrigation technologies are another important step forward. The use of drip irrigation, for example, is dramatically reducing both the amount of water needed for crops and the amount of chemicals, especially fertilizers, put into the soil. At the same time, this type of system increases crop yields while cutting costs by reducing the need for expensive chemicals and labor. In almond fields in California, drip irrigation often results in two to three times the per-acre tonnage at harvest time while requiring about half as much water as traditionally irrigated fields.[15]

In Denmark, the Ministry of Food, Agriculture and Fisheries has announced an action plan with an immediate goal of converting 10 percent of the country's agricultural production to organic farming and a long-term goal of 100 percent conversion. In the United States, it is the consumer who is driving the change. Retail sales of organic products in this country increased by 20 percent or more each year from 1990 through 1997. The U.S. Department of Agriculture—which has an embarrassingly small eleven-person staff for its organic farming program—predicts that sales of organically grown produce will exceed $10 billion by 2002. The organic farming market has made the transition from niche to mainstream.[16]

The second step in solving the country's food production problems is to encourage and support small agricultural operations and family farms. Small farms are best suited to organic agriculture, but there is still a need for education of farmers and would-be farmers in the skills and theory required to make this kind of farming a success. The national Organic Trade Association, with more than 500 organic business members, is now providing such services. Planning of communities so that farmable lands are maintained as agricultural greenbelts will create an opportunity for sustainable agriculture to get a foothold and at the same time assure the communities of continued local food production.[17]

The third step is for people to grow more of their own food. A 1994 study undertaken in the United Kingdom revealed that production of 10 liters of orange juice consumes 1 liter of diesel fuel for processing and transport and 220 liters of water for irrigation and for washing the fruit.[18] Compare these environmental and economic costs to that of stepping out the door, picking the oranges from your own yard, and squeezing fresh juice from them.

How can we bring about all three of these steps? We can design our communities so that food production can take place at a number of levels: the individual household or group of households, the neighborhood community, the town as a whole, and the small neighboring farm.

Production at the household level is the most ecologically sound in terms of saving energy and also in terms of using space efficiently. Vegetable gardens, herbs, fruit and nut trees, and grapevines can be integrated into private yards and small common areas to serve many of the same purposes of purely ornamental landscaping. Even a household with little interest in agricultural projects can enjoy the benefits of low-maintenance fruit trees and grapevines. Chickens or rabbits can be raised in a small space and fed partly with kitchen scraps and lawn trimmings. Their manure, together with garden waste, yields compost of great value as a mulch and fertilizer. Most households that make a serious effort at food production can supply a significant portion of their food needs on residential lots of average size. It is interesting to note that the city of San Francisco's sustainability plan, adopted in 1997, encourages the planting of a fruit tree in every yard.

Even in northern and high-altitude climates, use of a well-designed solar greenhouse can provide good, fresh cool-weather vegetables all winter long. During the cooler months, commercial produce is likely to be high in price and low in quality, due partly to the extra transportation and handling required to import it from warmer regions still in production. If the greenhouse is attached to the home, it can reduce heating bills by donating some of its solar-heated air to the rest of the house, especially on cold but sunny days.

A group of households can arrange to plant trees and vines with varied ripening dates in individual yards or in a common area and share the produce so that everyone will have a constant supply of ripe fruit in season and some left over to preserve for the rest of the year. Chickens or rabbits can also be raised as a group project; many times, such cooperative efforts can save time and space.

Either way, this smallest-scale agriculture provides an opportunity for community interaction. As a group project, it requires consultation and cooperation among households. As an individual household project, it often yields surpluses to share with the neighbors, and this, too, provides occasions for social contact.

Agriculture at the neighborhood community level offers a different set of advantages. Like private yards, neighborhood open spaces reduce density, provide visual variety, and can be landscaped with plants that produce food. In many climates, such plants as *Rosa rugosa* (a type of rose that produces large rose hips used for culinary purposes.) blueberry, and pineapple guava can be used as ornamental shrubs; nut trees can be used for shade and orna-

mental value. Orchard, vineyard, and vegetable crops can be planted as border barriers or for landscape relief. Other plants usually considered purely
ornamental can provide forage for bees.

Beekeeping has two very important functions in the community. The
first is to pollinate crops. Without an adequate population of bees, production of many fruits and vegetables is lowered drastically. The second function is production of honey, which can be used in place of sugar.

Food processing, such as drying of fruit, shelling of nuts, and food storage, can often be done more conveniently and economically at the neighborhood community level because it requires equipment and facilities that a
household or group of households could neither afford nor fully use. In
many instances, the neighborhood community can maintain root and fruit
cellars, frozen storage, and dry storage at a much lower cost per household
than if each household provided its own.

Agriculture at the neighborhood community level provides jobs for a few
agricultural workers and gives them a visible and respected place in the community. It also creates opportunities for children to become involved in the
food production process with part-time jobs; this not only is educational but
also gives them a healthy sense of self-esteem by allowing them to make a
real contribution to their families and their neighborhood.

A somewhat new idea that emerged in the 1960s in Japan is that of the

*The children of Village Homes help harvest
almonds.*

subscription farm, also known as community-supported agriculture. Local farmers, usually organic farmers, sign up consumers to purchase a certain amount of produce every week. In this way, the farmer is guaranteed a market for his or her products and the consumer receives fresh, wholesome, locally grown produce. This system has been incorporated in Prairie Crossing, a new, ecologically responsive neighborhood of 317 homes near Chicago where 350 acres are devoted to open space and some of that area is used as a community farm. Residents pay a subscription fee to purchase the fruit and vegetables grown there.

Another idea that has been around for some time is that of the community garden. The city of Seattle's Department of Neighborhoods, among other local government agencies, now has a program that helps neighborhoods develop community gardens by providing technical assistance and matching funds. This not only assures residents of fresh food but also helps create a sense of community.

In Village Homes, food production is part of the neighborhood and the lifestyle. A case study in the potential for integrating food production into the neighborhood, Village Homes demonstrates that the idea is both feasible and marketable. Homes in the community are always in demand.

Agriculture surrounding a town or city should aim to fill the gaps left by household and neighborhood community food production. Local farms should supply food for the city's markets and restaurants.

In Berkeley in the 1980s, Alice Waters began mentioning the names of her purveyors on the menu of her famed Chez Panisse restaurant. Vegetable growers, cheese makers, and bread bakers were all noted as she championed the virtues of eating locally produced food. The trend caught on, and many restaurants in the United States now use products that are locally produced and acknowledge the local producers.[19]

One way to ensure that priority is given to food production for local use and to prevent the use of dangerous chemicals or other practices not in the public's best interest is for a town to own agricultural greenbelts within its borders and lease the land to individual farmers. The leases could be extended for as long as the land is properly cared for and its productivity maintained.

If possible, agriculture should extend beyond the circumference of the town. A mixture of forest, grain crops, dairies, poultry farms, orchards, and vineyards can create a beautiful setting for the perimeter of a town. Forests can supply grazing land, wood for energy, and the natural setting necessary for human fulfillment. Grain crops can provide food for people and animals. Dairies and poultry farms can efficiently supply the town with their products. Creating an agricultural greenbelt around a town or city through zoning is an essential step. Davis's neighboring cities of Vacaville and Dixon have adopted this strategy: they purchased land between the two city's borders and are leasing it for farming.

In general, the agricultural policy of a community should be formulated to help small, family-size farms remain profitable, rebuilding the traditional relationships between the town and the small-scale local farmer. Farmers' markets play an important role in this regard by providing local farmers with a place to sell their produce.

Shelter

Shelter is another of the basic human needs, protecting people and their belongings from variable weather conditions. It also offers protection from intruders, indicates territorial bounds, and provides a sense of security. The use of shelter has permitted people to inhabit most of the earth's land surface, providing warmth in otherwise uninhabitable locations. It seems reasonable to believe that there is a basic predisposition that motivates people to obtain shelter, satisfying both physical necessity and psychological need. This predisposition results in a pattern of housing preferences that manifests itself in most cultures.

Most people have an innate desire to own a home. They want privacy, and they want their house to be connected to the earth, giving immediate access to the outside. They usually want the outside surroundings to be a part of the family's domain, whether it be a yard or a courtyard.

Other individuals adapted to a more urban environment prefer apartment living. A growing number of people desire cohousing, with its more communal lifestyle. This can involve individual houses or living units with additional shared facilities for cooking and eating and for general recreation.

Providing the type of housing people desire is easier said than done, especially today, with housing prices and the cost of construction increasing faster than wages. Many moderate-income families and almost all lower-income families have been priced out of the homeownership market. Unless they have owned their home for years, they must rent. The most promising solution for these people lies in returning to the owner-builder or self-help method by which people once built their own shelters. This requires a large investment of time and energy—often greater than one imagines at the outset—but the benefits of emotional satisfaction and the opportunity to own one's own home or to build superior-quality and special, personalized features into one's house often make the investment worthwhile.

Some small-scale owner-builder projects have been under way for a number of years. For example, with money from the U.S. Department of Agriculture's Rural Development mission area, previously known as the Farmers Home Administration, and other lending institutions, the Rural California Housing Corporation continues to provide new homes for lower-income families. The corporation purchases lots in rural areas or cities with fewer than 20,000 persons. Eight to ten qualified families are organized, loans are negotiated, and a work schedule is arranged.

Each group of families goes to work under a company team leader, who supervises each phase of the construction and determines which jobs, such as wiring, should be done by professionals. Each family is required to work a minimum of thirty hours per week. In the early stages of construction, the entire group pours concrete foundation slabs, places framing, and nails roof beams. Later, families do the finish work on their individual homes. It generally takes eight to twelve months to complete each set of homes.

As mentioned previously, in Village Homes we provided a program geared to help low-income people build their own houses. They performed enough work during evenings and weekends to earn the down payments for their houses. Construction took about seven months. By the end of this

Children of a former migrant farmworker pose in front of the house their father built in Village Homes.

period, the people in the program had acquired skills that allowed them to find jobs that paid much better than those they had held before entering the program. Members of the seven families that went through the program were extremely happy to move into a stable housing situation; they like the neighborhood and feel more secure with their new jobs. The children of several families of migrant farmworkers had the opportunity to get the education necessary to break out of the low-income lifestyle for which they had previously seemed destined.

For us, the most difficult part of carrying out the program was obtaining home loans for our owner-builders. We initially thought that the California Housing Finance Agency would be able to help; however, the agency seemed as lacking in innovation as the banks. Finally, a small local bank—which has since sold out to a larger conglomerate—provided the loans. However, we never were able to get the number of homes financed for low-income residents that we had initially planned.

We considered pursuing federal Housing and Urban Development (HUD) "section 8" financing through a federal program in place at the time. However, along with the federal program came federal mandates with which our established residents were uncomfortable, particularly the requirement that the federally supported housing be marketed to low-income people outside the city of Davis. At a meeting in our home, we learned from our initially disgruntled neighbors that it was not low-income families they were afraid of; it was intrusion of federal programs into their community. The neighbors pledged that they would provide assistance to low-income families themselves—and in some cases, they did. Mexican farmworkers in the community who did not understand much English or U.S. tax forms received a great deal of support from, and established friendships with, their neighbors.

In 1989, the city of Davis established a policy requiring developers to set aside 6 percent of their lots for owner-builder programs. If more developers would undertake this type of self-help project, offering opportunities to low-income people who are willing to work and learn new skills, or if cities and counties would require developers to dedicate a certain percentage of their projects to owner-built housing, there would be far more benefits to the people involved and to society as a whole than can result from federally assisted rental programs.

Participation of new homeowners in construction of the neighborhood can also reduce housing costs by reducing the final price of building sites. The individuals involved in building should be allowed to go beyond simply building their houses. Involvement in building community facilities can also help reduce costs and create a sense of community. In Village Homes, residents were involved in the cooperative construction of community buildings, a swimming pool, paths and footbridges, fences, and such. There are other aspects of new communities that residents might help build or install, including water recycling facilities, utility systems, landscaping, energy generation systems, and even pedestrian and bicycle paths. All these projects could cut costs, making the housing more affordable and at the same time helping build community spirit.

Psychologist Eugene R. Streich conducted studies of people who lived in houses designed by Frank Lloyd Wright and reported that a group of people for whom Wright had designed a rural subdivision near Kalamazoo, Michigan, spoke very highly of their experiences in building their houses together. They ordered materials as a group to get lower prices and cooperated in the actual building process to make the job easier. There were picnics, recreational activities, and a generally friendly atmosphere. Several of the people, interviewed twenty years later, said that the time they spent building their homes together was one of the most enjoyable periods of their lives.[20]

All the measures discussed here to reduce the cost of housing reflect the way homes and communities have been created for most of the history of our society: local materials, owner-built dwellings, and neighborhood or community cooperation. It may be that even though we initially consider these options because of financial pressure exerted by a deteriorating economic climate, we will come to see that the ideas have merit in themselves. In fact, combining new, environmentally sound, small-scale technologies with old-fashioned community spirit and local self-reliance could be society's way out of the growing dilemma of unaffordable housing. However, housing experts say that deep subsidies will still be needed to house very low-income families in California.

Village Homes provides a mix of housing, from 2,800-square-foot homes, some occupied by physicians and other professionals, to one-bedroom cottages of 600 square feet built with retired people in mind, to one-bedroom apartment units. There are a total of 218 single-family homes, and about 20 percent of these are common-wall houses. Village Homes also has twenty-four apartment units, four of them built over offices, and one nine-bedroom co-op house, which we helped students build. The students provided the labor, and we provided guidance and a contractor's license. Now students and others can live there for $100 per month.

We were initially warned that providing houses for a mixture of income levels might lower the value of housing in the neighborhood; however, several recent studies document that mixing expensive housing with more

A co-op house in Village Homes, built by college students, provides an inexpensive place to live.

affordable housing has no negative effect on the value of the upper-end homes. We have certainly found this to be the case. Housing values in Village Homes have risen far more rapidly than have housing values in the rest of Davis, even though we have physicians living next door to former migrant farmworkers.

Over time, unfortunately, houses in Village Homes have been growing increasingly less affordable. Over a twenty-year period, the community's reputation has changed from "that hippie subdivision" to "the most costly place per square foot to live in Davis." Several of our owner-builders have left the neighborhood, selling their homes for a very large profit. Even very small houses are selling for a premium. Homes continue to be remodeled and expanded, increasing their square footage and their resale value. Our community offers a highly desirable, one-of-a-kind place to live, and this drives market values up. This problem will be solved only by building more neighborhoods like Village Homes.

Chapter 5

Society's Lifeblood: Energy

Life as we know it in the developed countries of the world depends on the use of energy supplies that will not last and the use of which has serious environmental consequences. For our communities to be sustainable, it is critical that we address this situation.

To understand the relationship of energy to modern civilization and industrial growth, it is important to recognize at least two distinct and very significant changes that occurred during the Industrial Revolution. The first was the burgeoning of applied technology that allowed people to satisfy their wants and needs in ways that could hardly have been imagined before. The second change was an exponential increase in the use of energy, particularly that from nonrenewable fossil-fuel sources—coal, oil, and natural gas. Before the Industrial Revolution, people relied almost exclusively on inexhaustible and renewable sources of energy—sunlight, wind and water power, and the burning of wood and other nonfossil fuels.

Although the second change followed the first, one should not assume that the growth of applied technology had to result in increased consumption of energy from nonrenewable sources. Had fossil fuels not been available, people would have found ways to do without them. Apart from high-temperature processes such as steelmaking that depended on coal, the Industrial Revolution could have been fueled with renewable energy. Windmills were used in the late eleventh century and early twelfth century and not only provided mechanical power but also greatly improved the living standards of women, freeing them from the dreary task of grinding grain by hand. Early factories did in fact use water power, and early steam engines burned wood. Hydroelectric generation once provided a great deal of our electricity. The shift to fossil fuels was a choice made on the basis of their temporary abundance and relatively low cost, once technology made it possible for us to drill and mine for them.

Similarly, our high per capita consumption of energy in general is not inextricably connected to our standard of living. It is the result of technological choices made in the past. Because energy was temporarily cheap and plentiful, we had little incentive to choose the energy-conserving alternatives. No one choice is to blame. Taken together, however, these policy decisions have led to continually increasing consumption of fossil fuels and have created the ominous threat of global climate change and a host of other environmental and economic problems.

For quite some time, forward-looking individuals have seen that this dependence is a dead-end road. We are running out of the easily recoverable fossil fuels that have been the mainstay of our high-energy technology.[1]

Christopher Flavin and Nicholas Lenssen of the Worldwatch Institute summed up the challenge before us:

> Scientists now estimate that the world will need to cut global carbon emissions to at least 60 percent below prevailing levels in order to stabilize atmospheric carbon dioxide at current concentrations. By contrast, the International Energy Agency now projects a nearly 50 percent increase in emissions between 1990 and 2010—most of it in the Third World, where per capita carbon emissions currently range from one twentieth to one fifth the level in industrial countries. To avoid the risk of potentially catastrophic climate shifts in the middle of the next century, when the human economy is expected to be several times larger, the world needs to achieve a rate of carbon emissions per dollar of gross world product that is roughly one tenth the current level. This essentially means an end to the fossil-fuel-based energy economy as we know it.[2]

The wisdom of a shift in energy supply priorities becomes evident with just a cursory review of a few more statistics. Petroleum reserves, at times seen as limitless, in fact are within a few generations of depletion. We are burning these fossil fuels at a rate equivalent to 175 million barrels of oil per day. Wasteful inefficiencies inherent in the process of fossil-fuel production yield on average only one-third of the fuel's energy; the rest literally goes up in smoke. The generation of electricity is a major source of carbon dioxide and other forms of air pollution. Throughout the world, it accounts for about one-third of all heat-trapping gases entering the atmosphere.

It has been obvious for years that we cannot depend indefinitely on the dwindling supply of fossil fuels for energy. Some still argue that we can switch to our vast reserves of coal or switch to nuclear energy when oil becomes scarce. However, both options hold peril.

Increased use of our coal reserves would pose serious environmental problems. Current levels of air pollution linked to the burning of coal and other fossil fuels already kill an estimated 50,000 people per year in the United States—a higher mortality rate than that associated with traffic accidents.[3] The potential dangers from nuclear energy are even more frightening because the United States has yet to come up with a credible plan for disposing of radioactive nuclear waste for the hundred or so nuclear power plants currently in operation. Our entire system of energy use has created external costs that we are passing on to future generations but that are not reflected in energy prices.

The problems and limitations of our energy consumption habits have become more clearly defined at the beginning of the new millennium. Fortunately, the solutions are just as clear. As early as the 1970s, Amory Lovins argued that we must move toward a more decentralized, sustainable energy program as quickly as possible. He called it the "soft path":

> We stand at a crossroads; without decisive action our options will slip away. Delay in energy conservation lets wasteful use run on so far that the logistical problems of catching up become insuperable. Delay in widely deploying diverse soft technologies pushes them so far into the future that any credible fossil fuel bridge to them has been burned: they must be well underway before the worst part of the oil and gas decline. Delay in building the fossil fuel bridge makes it too tenuous: what the sophisticated coal technologies can give us, in particular, will no longer mesh with our pattern of transitional needs as oil and gas dwindle.[4]

Denis Hayes, who directed the Solar Energy Research Institute during the 1970s and is now executive director of the Bullitt Foundation in Seattle, also argued that solar power is the best answer to our energy problem and warned of a new era of limits:

> Renewable energy sources—wind, water, biomass, and direct sunlight—hold substantial advantages over the alternatives. They add no heat to the global environment and produce no radioactive or weapons-grade materials. The carbon dioxide emitted by biomass systems in equilibrium will make no net contribution to atmospheric concentrations, since green plants will capture CO_2 at the same rate that it is being produced. Renewable energy sources can provide energy as heat, liquid or gaseous fuels, or electricity. And they lend themselves well to production and use in decentralized, autonomous facilities. However, such sources

are not the indefatigable genies sought by advocates of limitless energy growth. While renewable sources do expand the limits to energy growth, especially the physical limits, the fact that energy development has a ceiling cannot ultimately be denied.[5]

A sane energy policy would take into account the full costs of power sources and include the costs of military intervention and of damage to the environment in these calculations. When these factors are considered, it soon becomes clear that there is a large hidden price tag attached to cheap oil. Our fossil-fuel habit requires ongoing infusions of large sums of money to keep prices low. Taxpayers pay $25 billion every year to finance U.S. military operations in the Middle East. Another $20 billion or so from the same taxpayers goes to subsidize the cost of fossil fuels, artificially lowering prices that in turn encourage greater consumption. Add to that another $56 billion per year spent on oil imports. To get an estimate of the costs associated with air pollution damage on public health and our forests, waterways, and air quality, one can add another $150 billion to the total. [6]

It is estimated that the United States has spent more than $1 trillion since 1970 on importing foreign oil. Although we currently import approximately 50 percent of our oil, if current consumption patterns hold, we may be importing nearly all of it in less than two decades.

There are three steps we must take to move in the direction that was outlined so long ago but that has yet to be implemented and continues to be the challenge before us. First, we must continue to develop renewable and environmentally acceptable sources of energy. Second, we must continue to find ways to use energy much more efficiently and frugally as another form of conservation. Third, we must gradually restructure our economy and our society to minimize the need for operations and activities that demand energy, another form of conservation.

Moving toward Environmentally Acceptable, Renewable Energy Sources

Renewable energy sources provide about 20 percent of the world's total energy and about 8 percent of the total energy consumed in the United States. Wind power, the fastest-growing source of electricity in the world, is emerging as one of the least expensive means of generating electricity. In contrast, not a single new nuclear reactor has been ordered in the United States in more than a decade, whereas within the same period, more than six have been prematurely retired because of safety or economic concerns.

Some houses in Village Homes are warmed by skylights in winter. Almost all have solar water heaters.

Solar energy, including that embodied in wind, water currents, and biomass, has been used for thousands of years. Denis Hayes pointed out that "direct solar and its various indirect forms fit well into a political system that emphasizes decentralization, pluralism, and local control."[7] There is no better example of this than a solar home, where the owner can rely more on the sun for space heating and water heating than on the utility company.

In the 1970s, solar space heating began to take hold all over the United States as a method of heating housing and commercial buildings. Unfortunately, during the 1980s, with a drop in energy prices, the nation lost considerable environmental momentum in solar housing design and made little progress.

In Village Homes, we built more than fourteen different types of solar houses, demonstrating the effectiveness of a wide variety of systems and architectural styles. A study of utility bills in the community showed that the most simply designed solar homes, which cost almost no more than conventional homes, were achieving 40 to 50 percent solar heating, and many of the more sophisticated designs were getting as much as 85 percent.[8] The Village Homes recreation center gets almost all its winter space heating from rooftop solar panels, which heat water for the swimming pool during spring and fall.

Skylights brighten the interior of a Village Homes house in winter.

In Village Homes, solar panels heat the swimming pool in spring and fall and the community center in winter.

A greenhouse system heats one of the office buildings in Village Homes.

Solar water-heating systems, popular in the 1920s and 1930s, began reappearing throughout the United States in the 1970s, spurred by state and federal tax credits. In most parts of the country, solar water-heating systems in residential units are capable of producing 50 to 100 percent of domestic hot-water needs. In Village Homes, we have used three different systems and find that we get about 75 percent of our hot water from the sun by using forty-eight square feet of collector panels and an eighty-gallon tank.

Many states have introduced building codes that require more energy-efficient building design. Many of the new codes, such as California's, have resulted in dramatic cuts in energy use. By 1999, California's building and appliance standards, adopted in the early 1980s, were conserving more energy than could be produced by twelve large nuclear power plants.

SOLAR ELECTRICITY

Although it is not yet competitive with conventional sources except in certain niche markets, solar generation of electricity is seen as having great potential for large-scale power plants and even more potential for smaller units that would generate power for individual houses or housing developments.

Photovoltaic cells, which convert sunlight directly into electricity, are continually decreasing in cost. According to the Sacramento Municipal Utility District (SMUD) in California, which has led the nation in its commitment to the use and development of solar photovoltaic cells, the cost of most recent installations is less than $5 per watt and is dropping fast. Today, most solar photovoltaic panels cost about $40 per square foot and produce roughly $2 worth of electricity per square foot per year, based on wholesale bulk power prices. But in 2002, SMUD will be buying panels at a price equivalent to $12.50 per square foot. Housing tracts with rooftop solar cells in Sacramento and elsewhere have become small part-time solar power plants, selling their excess power during the day to the local utility company and buying it back again at night. Photovoltaic cells offer the greatest potential for small local generating facilities engaging in what is commonly referred to as distributed generation.

Companies such as BP Amoco, Enron Corporation, and Shell International Renewables are collectively investing about $1 billion in new facilities to produce state-of-the-art solar photovoltaic panels. Photovoltaic-generated electricity could be used to isolate hydrogen from water, producing a clean, renewable fuel for vehicles. Hydrogen fuels, though expensive, may be the most realistic in a future society that does not add additional carbon dioxide

Today, photovoltaic panels come in many shapes and sizes and are on the verge of being cost-competitive.

to the atmosphere. Other solar thermal generators already contributing power to California's energy grid use mirrors to focus the sun's heat on a boiler. The steam produced turns massive underground turbines to generate electricity.

HYDROELECTRIC GENERATION

Existing facilities for generation of hydroelectric power are among the cheapest nonpolluting sources of electricity. In the nineteenth century and in the first few decades of the twentieth century, water power made New England an industrial center. In fact, water power has produced a substantial amount of electricity across the country, generating 40 percent of the total in 1900,[9] though it accounts for less than 10 percent today.[10] Further increases in generating capacity will be determined as society weighs the value of the energy against the environmental effects of building more dams. Small-scale projects may still move forward at carefully screened sites. However, many potential large-scale projects may not be worth the adverse environmental effects they cause.

WIND GENERATION

Wind-powered electric generators were common on farms in the United States before rural power lines were built. Larger-capacity wind-powered generators now on the market produce electricity that costs less than 5 cents per kilowatt-hour, a price that is quite close to the going market rate for electricity generated from fossil fuels.

California was once home to more than 90 percent of the world's wind generating capacity. Due to an explosion of growth since the mid-1990s in countries such as Germany (which in 1997 surpassed California in total wind-generated electricity production), Denmark, and other countries in Europe, Asia, and South America, California's share of production has slipped to about one-tenth of the total world market. Although Germany now generates the most electricity from wind, the undisputed world leader is Denmark. This small peninsular country bordered by the windy North Sea derives about 8 percent of its electricity from wind power—far more than any other country. (California derives less than 1 percent of its electricity from the wind.)

Despite an impressive 22 percent average global growth rate for each year of the past decade, wind power supplies only a tiny fraction of the world's total energy supply. However, wind power is the most popular source of electricity for a growing number of "green" marketing programs being launched throughout the United States. In Colorado, for example, eight local governments and large corporations, such as Coors Brewing Company, have made the commitment to purchase a portion of their electricity from wind turbines being installed on the slopes of the Rocky Mountains.

BIOMASS

Biomass is a term used to describe renewable organic material—wood, agricultural waste, animal waste, garbage, and such—that can be used to generate energy. It is actually solar energy that has been stored through the process of photosynthesis. This energy can be converted to a variety of useful energy forms—hydrogen, charcoal, methane, and synthetic oils—with by-products usable as food, fertilizers, and chemicals.

In the mid-1800s, wood provided for more than 90 percent of energy needs in the United States; as late as 1940, it was still used for space heating in 20 percent of homes.[11] Although the use of wood for heating has almost ceased in recent decades, airtight stoves, particularly those of Scandinavian design, have influenced changes in stove designs in the United States that have helped make wood heating popular once again. Burning wood in the home in an airtight stove is far more efficient in terms of useful heat production than any system that involves converting wood to gas, alcohol, steam, or electricity at some central heating plant because less energy is lost in conversion and transmission.

Woodstoves are very appropriate in areas of low population density with much open space, where they will not produce high concentrations of carbon monoxide and particulate matter. Catalytic converters and new stove designs are further reducing the polluting effects of home wood burning for heat; in fact, catalytic converters are required in many densely populated areas. Wood can also be used on a larger scale to generate electricity for a community. Burlington, Vermont, a city of 40,000, was one of the first to take steps in this direction. Before 1977, Burlington bought most of its electricity from outside sources that used oil, coal, natural gas, or nuclear power to generate electricity. In that year, it refurbished its municipally owned ten-megawatt coal-fired generating plant and converted it to burn wood. The conversion, which boosted the plant's capacity to fifty megawatts, was a success.[12]

When operating at full capacity, the Burlington wood burner consumes approximately seventy-six tons of matchbook-sized wood chips each hour. Waste from nearby lumber, pulpwood, and firewood operations is hauled to the plant, chopped into chips, and fed into a large furnace that heats water to create steam to drive turbines. There is nothing unorthodox about the system; it merely burns wood instead of coal. In New England, wood is plentiful, and it is a renewable resource.

In California, more than fifty biomass plants were constructed in the 1980s and generated as much electricity as one large nuclear plant. These facilities not only produced power but also improved air quality because agricultural wastes previously burned in open fields were now generating electricity. The biomass plants also help local governments meet their goals for diversion of solid waste by eliminating the need to send urban and agricultural wood wastes to landfills. In addition, biomass plants help reduce forest fires because the wood fuel collectors remove dead wood and underbrush that could turn a small fire into a major catastrophe.

In another application of biomass technology, garbage and sewage are used to generate methane gas, which is then burned to generate electricity. For example, the Sacramento Municipal Utility District is working with the county of Sacramento to build an eight-megawatt power plant at the county landfill to provide "green" power for customers who are willing to pay more for clean electricity. The power plant will take advantage of methane that otherwise would be vented into the atmosphere and contribute to global warming.

Agricultural waste has also been used successfully in the production of transportation fuel. In Brazil, sugarcane waste is being used to produce alcohol to power cars, trucks, and buses. The cane waste is made into a mash, which is fermented, producing alcohol that can be distilled off. Wood chips and spoiled grain, fruit, and vegetables can also be used.

Geothermal Energy

Geothermal energy, not normally considered a solar derivative, is a site-specific resource whereby heat is drawn from the earth's interior to generate electricity and provide heat and steam for low-temperature applications. For thousands of years, hot springs have been used for bathing, heating, and ritual purposes. More recently, geothermal energy has been used to heat more than 11,000 homes in Reykjavík, Iceland.[13] Generation of electricity from geothermal sources dates back to the early 1900s in Larderello, Italy, and has subsequently been used in New Zealand, Japan, and parts of the United States.[14]

There are several basic types of geothermal energy, and the ways to harness them vary considerably. The most common system uses "dry steam" (primarily water vapor with no liquid) from the earth to power conventional generators. Wells are drilled to depths of 2,000 feet or more, tapping reservoirs of steam in the earth's crust. Dry steam is found in relatively few locations, however.

Geothermal energy can be used over a very wide spectrum of temperature and volume. At the low end of the spectrum, geothermal energy can heat and cool a single residence, a system in use in more than 100 buildings in the United States. Toward the high end of the spectrum, a single high-volume, high-temperature deposit of geothermal energy can be harnessed to generate electricity for a city of 1 million or more people.

Like other renewable energy technologies, geothermal energy production offers economic development benefits. An example can be seen in Imperial County, California, which has suffered from the highest unemployment rates in the state. In a county dominated by agriculture, the geothermal industry provides high-paying, stable jobs for more than 285 people, most of whom are local residents, amounting to more than $18.5 million in annual salaries and benefits. Moreover, the industry makes up 25 percent of the county tax base, producing more than $12 million in tax revenue each year for local government, schools, and special districts. (CalEnergy, the largest geothermal company in Imperial County, is the single largest county taxpayer each year.)

FUEL CELLS

A fuel cell is a device that converts the chemical energy of fuel directly into electricity. The fuel cell does not burn the fuel and does not produce steam. Instead, it relies on an electrical process that causes hydrogen atoms to give up their electrons.

Most current fuel cells are powered by natural gas, but other fuels, including hydrogen, can be used. Because of their modular form and short construction times, fuel cells are an ideal technology to be used in distributed generation applications. Their lack of emissions and their quiet, unobtrusive operation make them ideal candidates for urban use. In addition to the electricity produced by a fuel cell, the waste heat can be used in cogeneration, in which the same fuel produces both electricity and heat energy. A fuel cell has an overall efficiency rate of 82 percent instead of the 65 to 75 percent of traditional cogeneration systems.

Fuel cells are usually categorized by electrolyte type. Phosphoric acid, alkaline, molten carbonate, solid oxide, and proton membrane fuel cells are all under development or available on the market. Molten carbonate fuel cells are among the most promising. Their benefits include greater efficiency (90 percent instead of 82 percent) and availability of waste heat at higher temperatures, which opens up cogeneration potential for commercial and industrial applications.

Reducing the Need for Energy

Conversion to renewable energy sources will not entirely solve our energy problems. Unless we also learn to get along with less energy than we use today, we will find ourselves spending more and more of our income, directly and indirectly, for energy, and we will have less left for our other needs. If we hope to maintain our standard of living, we will have to find ways to use energy much more frugally and efficiently—ways to perform the same jobs with less energy.

A great deal of energy could be saved by use of electric appliances that operate with less power. Household appliances are now being designed to use electricity more efficiently. For example, replacing an old refrigerator with a new energy-efficient model can reduce electric bills by $1,500 over six to eight years.

A household that buys equipment and appliances that carry the Energy Star, a label established by the U.S. Department of Energy and the Environmental Protection Agency to certify that a product meets energy efficiency standards, prevents the release of 70,000 pounds of carbon dioxide over the lifetime of the typical equipment and appliances used in any home. Carbon dioxide is the primary culprit in today's global climate change crisis. Use of Energy Star products cuts by nearly half the release of nitrogen oxides, air pollutants that are primary contributors to smog and acid rain.

Businesses also benefit immensely from energy efficiency. Consider these statistics:

- Simply turning off photocopiers at night and on weekends can reduce energy use by 65 percent.
- Turning off personal computers when they are not in use can cut energy consumption by 75 percent.
- Energy-efficient laser printers can cut energy consumption by more than 60 percent.
- Thermal fax machines use 30 percent less energy than do laser fax machines.

These simple changes in habits and purchases can pay off. For example, IBM Corporation estimated that it saved $17.8 million worldwide in a single year by encouraging employees to turn off equipment and lights when not in use.

A number of cities and counties in the United States have taken dramatic steps to reduce the energy requirements of buildings. The conservation measures required are quite simple but effective: insulating ceilings and water heaters, caulking and weather-stripping windows, installing energy-use meters, and replacing gas pilot lights with electric ignition devices. Lighting is the largest electric expense for local governments, constituting 45 percent of the average local government's electric bill, according to the California Energy Commission. The city of San Jose replaced lamps and ballasts with more energy-efficient equipment as part of the local utility's Power Savings Partners program. The city now saves $200,000 annually under this program.

Even high-rise buildings are undergoing design changes to cut down on energy costs, which have risen to account for nearly one-third of total building operating costs. Houses may also be designed and oriented to reduce or eliminate the need for conventional heating and cooling, as was done in Village Homes. Natural cooling is accomplished in Village Homes by capturing cool breezes that come from the south. Windows, which are equipped with burglar-proof ventilation locks that allow them to stay open but not wide enough for anyone to climb in, allow a flow of air through the house all night. This cools down the high-mass materials in the well-insulated houses enough to keep them cool all day, when the houses are closed up.

One way local governments can reduce energy use is by issuing local energy efficiency guidelines for new housing developments. For example, in California, under a program of the Local Government Commission called the Local Energy Assistance Program (LEAP), energy efficiency experts reviewed plans for 145 new single-family homes in Escalon, a small city in the Central Valley. It was discovered that changing the lot orientation so that homes face south would collectively save residents a total of $1,734 per year. If the city or developer planted trees in the street, the savings would increase to $4,126 per year. Addition of a few energy efficiency measures in the houses could increase the annual energy savings of the project as a whole to $10,527. On the basis of these numbers, the city council approved our suggested changes in the project.

All of these conservation measures are aimed at reducing our energy consumption without substantially changing the way we conduct our lives. At the same time, however, we should look at how we could change our lifestyles to eliminate energy use altogether where it is not really necessary.

In recent years, energy has been so inexpensive that we have used it to do more and more of the work we used to do for ourselves. Technology has provided us with some outstanding labor-saving devices that greatly enhance our lives. But it has also given us a plethora of gadgets whose appeal may be based more on their novelty than on any real usefulness.

As a society, we need to develop an ethical awareness of and opposition to such waste so that people will simply avoid buying or using unnecessary gadgets. Garbage disposals, for example, can be eliminated, and the good organic material that typically goes down the drain can be put to better use by composting and recycling it back into the garden. Clothes can be effectively dried outdoors on a clothesline or, in bad weather, indoors on drying racks. Since the advent of cheap electricity, we have learned to consider clotheslines and drying racks unsightly, but when designed into a house or yard as standard elements, they can be quite unobtrusive.

With regard to transportation, we can all try to walk or bicycle whenever possible rather than drive, and we can organize our time and our errands so that when driving is necessary, we accomplish many things in one trip. Because of the enormous amount of energy used in personal transportation, designing cities to be built on a scale at which walking and bicycling are convenient can be one of the greatest energy savers of all.

Restructuring for a Low-Energy Society

Given new technologies, it is now possible to make a house a net energy producer by using superior insulation techniques and installing a solar water heating system and solar photovoltaic roof tiles. But even if every house were constructed in this manner, we would still be using a large amount of energy to transport people and freight. Currently, we are using approximately 25 percent of our energy for these purposes. Conservation can cut our energy consumption, but with a growing population, overall energy consumption will inevitably increase.

In the future, energy for transportation could come from our dwindling oil supplies, natural gas, or synthetic fuels made from coal. None of these solutions, however, addresses the long-range problem of carbon dioxide buildup, and they all will be very expensive in terms of money and adverse environmental effects.

The solar alternative for running vehicles—on electricity from photovoltaic cells and wind generators, on hydrogen generated from photovoltaic electric current, or on alcohol produced by biomass—will not have the enormous environmental cost but will be very expensive. The most realistic long-range answer will be to both utilize these new technologies and reduce much of the need for transportation through better and more efficient urban design.

The present urban structure, which requires a high energy input to function, evolved without the constraints of global climate change and today's growing awareness of the negative effects of fossil-fuel development on drilling and excavation sites. We must restructure our cities for the long run. John and Nancy Todd of the New Alchemy Institute put it this way:

> If it is assumed that making adjustments with parts of the total system is only buying time, the vital support elements of our society must be totally redesigned. For a transition to take place, the new process being created must be allowed to coexist within the present structure.[15]

Now, perhaps for the first time in history, people are being asked to create the landscape of the future. There will be little time for the slow adaptation of techniques that has in the past characterized change in human experience. The central task now is to find an adaptive structure in which individuals have a wide range of opportunities within environmental and social contexts that enhance the whole society.

There are a number of ways in which we can begin to change the present high-energy urban structure:

- To facilitate the use of renewable energy sources, we should locate new development in areas where those sources are most plentiful.

- To eliminate the need for much of the energy now consumed by automobiles and trucks, we can design our neighborhoods and cities (including production and distribution systems) in such a way that the need for these kinds of transportation is minimized.

- Neighborhoods should provide maximum convenience for pedestrian and bicycle traffic with paths that connect all parts of the neighborhood. Automobile routes through the neighborhood should be minimized.

- To further reduce the need for driving, commercial and public facilities should be integrated. Residential areas should be kept within one-half mile to one and one-fourth miles from the town center, which should be rich in entertainment and commercial variety.

- Schools should be kept within one-half mile of all homes. Convenience stores and other services should be strategically located close to all neighborhoods. Baskets and trailers on bicycles can be used for carrying children and packages, and very small enclosed-pedal or electric vehicles (with maximum speeds of six or seven miles per hour) may provide workable alternatives for elderly people or for general use in severe climates.

In a town designed and built to include these features, the convenience normally associated only with the automobile will cease to exist. The automobile not only will lose importance as a means of transportation within the neighborhood and town but also may actually become an inconvenient way to get around.

Regional mass transit systems could also be more efficiently organized if our urban sprawl were broken up into new towns and rehabilitated suburban areas. Buses or trains could link the centers of towns with trams or buses that make local runs from town centers into the neighborhoods. The more convenient regional transit is, the more it will be used.

Portland, Oregon, which has a jump start on this idea, has experienced a total of $1.9 billion worth of development immediately adjacent to its light-rail line since the decision was made to construct the transit system. Plans have been announced for another $0.5 billion worth of transit-oriented development.[16]

There are many other ways in which town planning can save energy in the nonresidential sector. Low crime rates resulting from well-designed communities can reduce the amount of fuel used by patrolling police. As in Davis, bike path systems can allow bicycles to be used as part of the police patrol system. Centralized commercial areas can cut down on energy used by delivery trucks and vans. More food and other consumer goods can be produced locally, cutting down on long-haul transportation energy expense. Locating some businesses and industries in each neighborhood can also provide employment and reduce the number of people commuting.

In making the transition to environmentally sound, renewable energy sources, conservation and better design must become priorities for every individual, for each community, and for the country as a whole. Barry Commoner, an independent candidate for U.S. president in 1980, said back in 1979:

> As a non-renewable energy source is depleted, it becomes progressively more costly to produce, so that continued reliance on it means an unending escalation in price. This process has a powerful inflationary impact: it increases the cost of living, especially of poor people; it aggravates unemployment; it reduces the availability of capital. No economic system can withstand such pressures indefinitely; sooner or later the energy crisis must be solved. And this can be done only by replacing the present non-renewable sources—oil, natural gas, coal, and uranium—with renewable ones which are stable in cost. That is what a national energy policy must do if it is to solve the energy crisis, rather than delay it or make it worse.[17]

Although the federal government, if it so chooses, can help the transition to solar power to occur in an orderly and expedient manner by providing helpful legislation, it will ultimately be up to the individual and the community to make the change. There are few incentives for the large energy corporations we have relied on in the past to assist us in becoming self-reliant in terms of energy. In fact, it is most likely that there will be an ongoing political and economic battle, with the government in the center, over whether we should have locally produced energy on a small scale or coal and nuclear power produced by large industries.

Chapter 6

The Use of Resources in Sustainable Design

It is important for each community and region to have its own safe and dependable supplies of water, food, and energy and to provide shelter for all its residents. To be sustainable, each community or region should also have control and ownership of its land and resources. It should produce enough goods and services for export to equal what it imports, and it should make efficient use of local resources through conservation, reuse, and recycling. Otherwise, the community will be economically weak and vulnerable to changes in supply and demand that are entirely outside its control.

One example of what can happen to a region that does not control its own resources, exports all that it produces, and imports all that it consumes is the situation in some of the coal-mining communities in Appalachia. There, the community's local resource is coal. The coal is owned by outside interests, so the profits are spent outside the community. It is true that the workers' salaries bring money into the community, but they do not represent the value of what the community is producing. A large percentage of the people work in the mines, so very few of the products the community consumes are produced in the community. Therefore, most of the money that people earn by working at the mine must be spent on importing goods and services.

This leaves the community in an extremely weak position because anything that stops coal production also stops the community's major source of income, bringing the already weak local economy to a grinding halt. This is not a hypothetical situation; it has happened over and over in the lives of many people living in communities dependent mainly on one form of industry, especially when that industry is owned by outside interests.

In any of these localities, the situation would be totally different if the community were more diversified in its industry and production and if the industry's profits were retained in the community. Many of the Appalachian communities, rich in resources, water, and energy and with reasonably good growing seasons, could be prosperous and economically stable communities if those changes were made.

Building more self-sufficiency into our local economies not only is of value to the people who live in them but also is an important step in achieving national security and ecological stability. With a productive system that is decentralized in the sense that local communities are able to produce a high percentage of their basic needs and that is centralized in the sense that the overall economy produces a variety of more specialized goods and services that are exchanged throughout the system, the United States could maintain reasonable stability during a major economic or environmental disruption. Our present centralized system can handle an emergency such as a localized disaster by providing relief from outside, but a more decentralized system would have an advantage during major disruptions such as a nationwide energy shortage or drought. In these cases, most localities would still be able to produce the essentials and maintain reasonable economic production even if the problem were of fairly long duration.

Another important advantage of having more self-reliant communities is that more of the decisions that affect people's lives can be made locally, giving people more choices that represent real freedom. People will have more freedom to choose how their resources are used, what kinds of working conditions are acceptable, what energy supplies are used, and what environmental consequences are acceptable. When there is more local control, votes and voices have much more significance; when we can personally speak with the owner of a business, we have more ability to persuade.

Writer and social critic Richard J. Barnet suggested:

> In the United States, we could start by redefining "national security" to make the security of local communities and regions a prime national goal. Locally raised tax money should be used to develop community-based energy systems, development banks, and other institutions to revitalize local economies. Our national policy should be designed to enable communities to undertake a variety of such initiatives.[1]

The following is a further discussion of the importance of community control of land and resources, local production of goods and services, local generation of energy, and efficient use of resources through conservation, reuse, and recycling. Also provided are a few examples of related individual actions and policy changes that can lead every community in the United States to a more sustainable existence.

Land and Resources

The land and its rich supply of resources are the physical foundation of our society. Our food comes from the land, and we use the earth's resources to build our houses and cities and to make the products that help us live from day to day.

For a population to survive, it must have access to the land and its resources, and for it to flourish, the land and resources must be rich and plentiful. If the population is to sustain itself for more than a short duration, it must maintain the renewable resources in good condition and it must not deplete the nonrenewable resources.

Land and resources are the basis of wealth. A modest accumulation by an individual, community, or country helps to ensure stability and survival. A large or disproportionate accumulation, however, enables disproportionate power and control.

Throughout history, empires have been built by military takeovers of people and their lands. Fortune after fortune has been amassed by the shrewd maneuvering of individuals as they gain control over other individuals, land, and resources. The struggle for control of the power that wealth provides has probably caused more human suffering than anything else, with the dislocation of people from their lands by either war or economic reasons causing the greatest suffering. Richard Barnet makes the point:

> The fact that people are hungry is due less to insufficient food production than to maldistribution. Most people who are forced to stop eating do so not because there is insufficient food grown in the world but because they no longer grow it themselves and do not have the money to buy it.[2]

Even if a population does not starve from lack of control over land and resources, its freedom is certainly diminished, along with the quality of individual lives. The following is a discussion of some of the many instances in which people's lives are impoverished by lack of land and resources.

Professor Walter Goldschmidt, in his 1946 study of the California farming cities of Dinuba and Arvin, indicated that where large agribusiness concerns had taken over most of the land around a community, buying it up from small farmers who could no longer afford to maintain it, the quality of life for most members of the community decreased.[3] These findings are further supported by a report of rural community life by Professor Dean Mac-Cannell of the University of California, Davis. His report states:

> In areas such as the Westlands and the Imperial Valley of California, where giant corporate operations are the norm, we find poverty, inequality, ignorance, and a full range of related social pathologies.[4]

The report indicates that as a result of a federal water project intended to help family farms, large agribusiness benefited instead by purchasing large tracts of land and farming them. This happened because of lack of enforcement of a 1902 law designed to protect small farmers by limiting the amount of water drawn from federal water projects to 160 acres per customer.

Perhaps the most glaring example of what can happen to a group of people when they are deprived of their resources is that of the Native American people who live on reservations. Their rights to their land and resources have been taken from them. The land they live on and the resources on the land usually are not theirs to use as they see fit; they are held in guardianship for them by the federal government. If they want to do something with the land or its resources, usually they must go through months of bureaucratic red tape, often only to receive a denial of their request. This inability to have control over their lives has left many of them apathetic and almost all of them dependent on the federal government. One wonders whether this may be the reason why rates of alcoholism and suicide are higher for Native Americans living on reservations than for any other segment of the U.S. population. Conversely, where they have regained control over their land and resources, Native American communities have begun to prosper.

Many minority communities in the ghettos of our cities are without land and resources and are largely dependent on the federal government. Their communities have no economic base, and again, severe social problems exist. For most people in the United States, these cases may seem unusual and of no direct concern. But we should be concerned. The more our land and resources are bought up by multinational corporations, the more they are out of our control and the less choice we have as individuals and communities. The disenfranchised population at the bottom is continuing to grow at the same time wealth is being amassed at the top.

We can begin to change this trend if we are careful in both the way we carry out our business and the way we structure our cities and our local economies. We can support small local businesses that supply materials from their own holdings, such as timber companies or mills, cement producers, gravel quarries, farmers, tile-manufacturing companies, and so on. Communities can form investment corporations to amass enough money to buy holdings of resources, or they can jointly purchase resources needed to sustain some of their local industries. When new development is planned, a certain amount of land can be set aside for food production or energy supply from forests. Moreover, communities can be spaced far enough apart for land and resources to be located around them, giving more opportunity for local business to operate at a smaller scale. In this day and age, it is impossible for a community to provide the full range of resources it needs. However, by owning a substantial amount of some important resources, a community can increase its economic stability.

The next step an individual or community can take is to build with materials that are as durable as possible so that they do not need to be replaced. Short-term savings that come from buying less durable products do not add to a community's stability if the community must continually rely on outside sources to replace those products. Buildings and roads must last. The use of concrete for paving is an example of this principle. In many cases, concrete can be expected to last for 100 years or more, whereas asphalt must be repaved every 10 to 15 years. Asphalt requires more sophisticated technology than cement and lends itself more to centralization. Durable building materials such as tile for floors are superior to materials that must be replaced periodically, and tile can be produced locally by a small business.

Resources must be conserved in the community, soils maintained and improved, and forests reestablished. Throughout history, where this has not been practiced, the resulting lack of resources and decline in quality of land has led to the decline of civilizations.

It is clear that a community's ability to control its own energy, food, shelter, and water depends largely on its ability to control a significant amount of land and resources. This can be achieved through small local businesses, community-based corporations, or public ownership of some of the land, which is then leased to private businesses. Clearly, it is up to the members of a community to ensure that the community has the resources and land necessary for a strong economic base. In Village Homes, this has been carried out in a small way through community ownership of the commercial center, agricultural lands, and income-producing apartment units.

Goods and Services

One cannot speak of the goods and services necessary for a community without speaking of the nature of the occupations that produce them. The quality of the goods and services and their value to society should be considered

equally with the laborers who produce them, the environmental consequences of their production, the way they are used, and their economic
effect on the community.

Economic activity should satisfy or at least be consistent with the satisfaction of people's social and psychological needs. Work should take place in
a pleasant environment not too far away or too separate from the workers'
community life. This does not necessarily mean less efficient production; but
even if it does require some sacrifice in productivity, such as a switch to
smaller-scale production, it is worth it. Production is not an end in itself.
Goods and services are valuable only because they satisfy human needs. It
makes no sense to sacrifice human values in the workplace for a few more
goods and services.

Many productive enterprises now carried out by large, impersonal centralized businesses could be handled just as well by small, friendly local businesses. In France and other European countries, fresh, wholesome baked
goods and cold meats are still produced by neighborhood bakeries and char-
cuteries instead of by a few large manufacturers. Clothing and furniture can
also be produced efficiently on a fairly small scale.

Locally owned businesses contribute to the economic health and sustainability of the community. Their profits are recycled within the city in
which they are located. According to Kennedy Lawson Smith, director of the
National Main Street Center of the National Trust for Historic Preservation,
locally owned small businesses return about 60 percent of their profits to the
community, whereas chain stores return about 20 percent and discount
superstores about 5 to 8 percent.

A return to decentralization and smaller businesses paves the way for a
return to direct marketing. This has its own advantages of creating more satisfying human interaction and reducing costs by eliminating the need for
wholesalers and warehouses. Farmers who market their own produce and
craftspeople who sell or deliver directly from their shops or homes are the
most efficient and energy-conserving distributors.

In his study of direct marketing, University of California professor
Robert Sommer observed that in farmers' markets, prices are lower and food
is fresher. But beyond that, there are social advantages: "A farmers' market is
a community event. It is a place where people congregate and exchange ideas
and talk 'neighborhood' and politics. By contrast, the supermarket is a sterile and desocializing environment."[5]

Sommer notes that direct marketing is beginning to enjoy a renaissance.
In the early 1970s, for example, Massachusetts did not have a single farmers'

Farmers' markets are growing more popular.

market; by 1980, there were thirty of them in operation. Now, farmers' markets are found everywhere across the United States.

Suffering from the erosion of resource-extraction industries such as timber harvesting, the environmentally and socially conscious rural community of Arcata, California, was stereotyped as "antibusiness." But by encouraging local entrepreneurs to build small businesses, the city ended up featured in *Inc.* magazine and the *Wall Street Journal*. Not only do Arcata's local businesses thrive; many have also become international exporters of unique products.

One exceptional effort in Arcata is a city-funded "business incubator" that helps local entrepreneurs add value to locally grown crops. The incubator serves small businesses in the food industry, those that manufacture specialty syrups, jams and jellies, and the like. The owners of these businesses are now encouraging local farmers to grow crops organically because organic foods have higher economic value. The incubator is also helping the businesses market their wares jointly through Christmas catalogs, and the businesses are beginning to broaden their sales through use of the Internet.[6]

Arcata's business incubator serves as an example of how a local government can assist small businesses through special economic development programs. However, planning and zoning are equally important. Neighborhood centers that provide space for small businesses and local ordinances that allow home-based businesses are of critical importance in providing an appropriate setting.

Policies that support the traditional downtown rather than the shopping mall also help local businesses. A mall is usually operated by an owner of a number of malls geared for chain businesses that are affiliated with multinational corporations. Not only are these businesses not locally owned, but also

The city of Hanford, California, successfully revitalized its downtown area. (Photographs courtesy of the city of Hanford, California)

the majority of their products are produced by corporate subsidiaries or affiliates. In contrast, the scale and ownership patterns of a subdivided downtown block are more suitable for locally owned businesses.

Fortunately, there is a strong movement today to revitalize America's downtowns. The National Main Street Center has been actively supporting this effort.[7]

Advocacy by new urbanists for incorporating town or neighborhood centers in their projects is also helping owners of small businesses. Haile Plantation, near Gainesville, Florida, is a particularly good example. The developer of this 1,700-acre master-planned community completed a one-third-mile-long Main Street as its centerpiece. This attractive, narrow, tree-shaded street is lined by more than forty buildings, including shops, a corner grocery store, a dry cleaner, a dentist's office, and a stockbroker's office.

As the United States moves from an industry-based economy to an information-based economy, the good news is that the number of small businesses is increasing. According to Doug Henton and Kim Walesh of Collaborative Economics, the new economic era will be dominated by small and medium-sized businesses, as opposed to the large businesses that dominated the industrial age. Already, more than 60 percent of the U.S. workforce is made up of employees of small firms, self-employed people, and part-time and temporary workers. Henton and Walesh view this as a new version of the crafts form of production. These businesses owners value the integration of work and home life and want their offices close to their homes. They value community and neighborhood centers as gathering places where they can network in an informal setting. They claim that this is critical for stimulating the creativity that allows them to maintain a competitive advantage in the new economy.[8]

In Village Homes, the community center is home to seventeen small businesses. Fifteen of these are owned by Village Homes residents, who walk or ride their bikes to work. Among them are a child-care center, a dance and exercise studio, a small restaurant that locally grows some of the vegetables on the menu, and offices of an environmental engineer, an architect, a dietitian, a massage therapist, a psychiatrist, several attorneys, two financial consultants, a graphic designer, an environmental advocacy group, and a corporate employee who telecommutes. Another building under construction will provide more office space with apartments above it.

Office space in the Village Homes community center is never vacant—there is always a waiting list of people anxious to move in. This, we believe, demonstrates that Henton and Walesh are correct in their analysis that the

There is always a waiting list for office space in Village Homes.

The Plumshire Inn in Village Homes—a delicious meal within walking distance.

U.S. economy is turning to a new version of arts and crafts production. It is in the best interest of communities to support this trend by providing appropriate, affordable, and convenient locations for small businesses.

The issue of sustainability aside, residents of Village Homes seem to place a high value on being able to integrate their home and family lives. Commuting to work via a short walk through a beautiful greenbelt rather than on a crowded freeway has an understandably strong appeal. Moreover, the increased security of the child who knows that his or her parents are within walking distance of school or home should not be undervalued.

In addition to providing space for small businesses to operate, communities of today need to invest in technology that supports the ability of local enterprises to succeed by providing open access to information and resources. This will become increasingly critical to economic vitality. The California Association for Local Economic Development points out:

> Telecommunications technology is changing dramatically the way business and government will be conducted. The need for telecommunications infrastructure such as rights of way, fiber optic lines and communications equipment will be as important as traditional locations factors (roads, sewers and water systems, etc.).[9]

Reduce, Reuse, Recycle

Nature is an excellent teacher of waste management policy. "First," it says, "forget the term *waste* and the mentality that goes with it. Second, take the by-products and end products that you used to call waste and reuse or recycle them all."

We should try hard to bring our activities into line with the dictum of nature (and of simple logic): "Waste not, reuse, and recycle." If we are producing any actual wastes—that is, products that cannot be recycled in some way—their buildup will eventually cause severe problems, threatening the environment, our health, and perhaps life itself. Waste products of this type should not be produced.

The tendency of our society to create unusable wastes and to neglect the recycling of materials that could be reused shows a basic, shortsighted irresponsibility, an attitude we must change if we want to maintain a reasonable quality of life and a livable environment. We are beginning to realize the importance of recycling, but our understanding needs to grow until we are fully aware that token or partial recycling will not suffice. All materials used by society must enter a continuous, circular path in which they undergo changes in form, ultimately becoming useful again after the passage of an appropriate length of time. Further, to maintain the health of the ecosystem, including human health, we must not produce substances whose existence threatens our well-being, even if these materials eventually degrade to harmless by-products. This includes cancer-causing pesticides, highly radioactive substances, and any other materials that eventually break down but whose intermediate by-products threaten the integrity of the ecosystem.

Society's life-support systems, including industries and their by-products, should be analyzed to make sure that the integrity of the ecosystem is maintained. Both the processing of raw materials and the disposal of end products should be done in ways that avoid environmental destruction, making maximum use of natural energy systems already operating in the environment. Besides solar and wind energy, these include tidal, geothermal, and magnetic energy forms as well as biological systems such as photosynthesis and bacterial transformations.

With these ideas in mind, let us now consider some specific types of waste and what is being done to reduce, reuse, and recycle them.

Sewage or wastewater, the used matter discharged into sewers and transported by water, is an important resource to consider for reuse and recycling. Sewage contains not only human excrement but also the residuals from sinks, baths, and laundry as well as industrial wastes and occasionally street runoff from storm sewers. The United States spends a great deal of money on disposal of sewage. The cost is high because of the energy and resources required to safely treat the wastewater according to standards set by local, state, and federal governments. Although these standards are necessary, the methods most communities use to attain them are questionable. There are components of sewage that are too valuable to be thrown away.

Many options exist for a community to adequately treat its sewage, recover valuable by-products, and reclaim the final effluent without consuming large amounts of energy. The number of options depends on the type of sewage to be treated.

Constructed marshes, also known as treatment wetlands, are becoming increasingly popular in wastewater treatment. After almost thirty years of use, these marshes now number more than 600 in North America. Unfortunately, the technology has not yet gained national regulatory acceptance, so projects are approved on a case-by-case basis.[10]

The city of Arcata's system, completed in 1986, has inspired much of the current popularity of constructed marshes. The system involves separating the city's sewage into wastewater and sludge. The sludge is dried, broken up, mixed with other organic materials, and spread across the city's soccer fields, in its forest, and on flower beds.

The wastewater has been used to create marshes, which have become an important asset to the city's tourism sector. Wastewater flows into a series of three marsh ponds, where plants draw bacteria and other toxins out of the water, and then it is released into Humboldt Bay. Every year, about 150,000 tourists flock to the town to visit the beautiful 154-acre Arcata Marsh and Wildlife Sanctuary and view the herons, egrets, pelicans, swallows, and other birds that live there. Most visitors are, of course, unaware that they are walking through a sewage treatment facility. The marsh is also a low-cost way to treat sewage—it saved the city more than $2 million compared with the price tag of a regional treatment plant. The designers of the system say that the marsh is really all about using what is at hand and getting the most out of resources.[11]

The efficiency of sewage treatment and the potential for wastewater reclamation and conversion of sludge to fertilizer depend primarily on the absence of toxic substances, heavy metals, and large quantities of salt in the sewage. Arcata's marsh works because the community has no heavy industry

Bird-watchers visiting the Arcata Marsh and Wildlife Sanctuary in Arcata, California, are generally unaware that it also serves as a sewage treatment facility. (Photograph courtesy of the city of Arcata, California)

and therefore there are few, if any, heavy metals in its sewage. Ideally, a community would also promote the use of household products that are compatible with sewage reclamation and prohibit by ordinance the use of household products that are detrimental. Homeowners wishing to use products that contaminate sewage—for instance, silver nitrate, which is a waste by-product of the film-developing process—would be required to install equipment to remove the harmful substances before they enter the sewer system.

There is much that industry can do to recycle or eliminate hazardous wastes and save money in the process. In the mid-1980s, the County of Ventura Environmental Health Department began providing technical assistance on waste reduction strategies to industries in the county. Among the achievements were the following:

- A 75 percent reduction in the volume of waste produced by an oil company. County personnel pointed out how a water conservation program could reduce the volume of contaminated water produced.

- A 90 percent reduction in the amount of hazardous waste sent by a pesticide formulator to landfill. County personnel recommended the installation of an activated carbon absorption unit to decontaminate rinse waters.

By reducing the amount of waste that had to be taken to a hazardous waste disposal facility, these companies dramatically reduced their costs.[12]

In terms of nonhazardous waste, considerable progress has been made since the construction of Village Homes. An example is the California Materials Exchange (CalMAX), a program initiated by the California Integrated Waste Management Board in the late 1980s. It is a statewide materials exchange program whereby businesses with unwanted materials can match up, through a regular publication or an on-line database, with businesses seeking materials. Similar, smaller programs exist throughout the country. These do a great deal to facilitate the reuse of building materials and the like.

A program in Berkeley, California, provides a locally based example. Urban Ore is a small business that salvages light fixtures, doors, windows, and other usable materials from old homes and sells them to individuals and home builders. All these efforts are assisted enormously by legislation in California that requires all cities and counties to reduce the amount of waste going to landfills by 50 percent by the year 2000. This law assures businesses that depend on reclaimed materials as feedstock that these materials will be available in adequate quantities.

The Official Recycled Products Guide also became available in the mid-1980s. It is a very successful national publication, produced annually, that provides information about where to obtain various products made of recycled materials. The publication lists a wide variety of building materials, from carpets to countertops, made from discarded plastics and other things that usually end up in landfills. Since its first publication, the number of entries in the guide has increased dramatically, indicating a substantial increase in the number and variety of products being produced from recycled materials.[13]

One exciting new product is a carpet that can be recycled, produced by Interface, Inc., in Atlanta, Georgia. According to the company's chairman and chief executive officer, Ray C. Anderson, "If successful, we'll spend the rest of our days harvesting yesterday's carpets, recycling old petro-chemicals into new materials, and converting sunlight into energy. There will be zero scrap going into landfills and zero emissions into the biosphere."[14] This business goes beyond recycling products to look at other ways it can reduce its negative effect on the environment. In 1994, Interface overhauled its environmental practices and corporate philosophy to take into account the total energy consumption and total waste of all its product lines. As a result, the company has documented its entire "environmental footprint" and set a baseline for reducing the company's adverse environmental effects, providing a cutting-edge model of how to operate a sustainable business. Interface has taken steps to eliminate waste, reduce toxic emissions, use renewable energy, close the recycling loop, reduce transportation, and educate consumers and redesign commerce. As has been our experience in Village Homes, sensitivity to the environment can provide financial dividends. Since implementation of these steps, Interface has saved an estimated $47 million, even as the company has increased production. The value of Interface stock has been skyrocketing.[15]

Another innovation is the ecoindustrial park, which brings together businesses that work together to lessen adverse environmental effects and, ideally, use one another's residuals as resources. Aside from efficiently recycling wastes, ecoindustrial parks promote economic development and save money. The first one was developed in the 1970s when five business partners got together to exchange materials and energy among themselves and others, including owners of small businesses and farmers. As of this writing, more than twenty ecoindustrial projects were in the planning stages in the United States, and a handful were expected to be operational by the end of 1999.[16]

The adage "Waste not, reuse, and recycle" should also apply in the design and construction of the buildings that make up our communities. In developing Village Homes, we attempted to ensure that we were using materials that would have a long life span. We used concrete roof tiles on every home and installed tile floors and countertops within the homes. Besides being durable, these have the added benefit of being high-mass materials that help to moderate temperature. We used concrete for the bike paths and parking bays because it lasts longer than asphalt. We also made a point of avoiding the use of toxic materials.

Since the construction of Village Homes, a whole new field of endeavor called "green building" has emerged. Advocates of this movement seek building materials that are not only long-lived but also locally produced, as in rammed earth and straw bale construction. They promote the reuse of salvaged building materials and the use of products that can be recycled or that are made of recycled materials. They focus on ensuring that the materials used in home construction are not toxic to either the home builder or the future inhabitants. In addition, they advocate methods discussed elsewhere in this book—daylighting (the use of natural light) and energy-efficient lighting, other energy efficiency measures, water conservation, and reuse and recycling.

The green building movement is in essence an advocacy group for sustainable development. The exciting and hopeful news is that it is promoted today not only by environmental organizations but also by organizations that are definitely in the "mainstream." The U.S. Green Building Council (USGBC), for example, is a coalition of more than 275 leading international organizations including manufacturers, building and design professionals, retailers, and financial industry leaders. Local governments are represented through Public Technology, Inc., the research, development, and commercialization arm of the National League of Cities, the National Association of Counties, and the International City/County Management Association. The USGBC has been instrumental in the development of voluntary standards used for guidance in the design and construction of buildings. The standards take into account energy and resource efficiency, handling of solid and hazardous wastes, and indoor environmental quality. The rating system goes beyond buildings to include the water efficiency of landscaping and drainage systems. The USGBC also gives credits to builders for providing bicycle parking facilities and for building on sites linked to mass transit.[17]

Always at the forefront, the city of Boulder, Colorado, in March 1997 adopted a program to require that building projects meet minimum "green standards" before being granted a permit. Projects receive points for environmentally responsible aspects of land use, framing, plumbing, utilities, energy use, and the like. Point requirements follow a sliding scale based on the project's size.

The most recent local government to take action is the city of Santa

Monica, California, which adopted its Green Building Design and Construction Guidelines in April 1999. These comprehensive guidelines recommend practices that reduce the ecological and resource-related effects of buildings and enhance the health and satisfaction of their occupants. The guidelines cover appropriate siting, landscape design, building design, building materials, electrical systems, heating and air-conditioning, and water systems. The city also requires a number of efficiency measures: buildings must exceed state energy efficiency standards by 20 to 30 percent, depending on the building type; storm-water runoff must be minimized through the use of permeable surfaces; storage must be provided for bicycles and recycled materials; solar collectors must be used to heat swimming pools and to preheat water in water heaters. When a building is demolished, salvageable materials must be recovered, and construction waste must be recycled. These controls have not discouraged businesses from locating in the city. Santa Monica has one of the strongest local economies in the state and a AAA bond rating.

Also of note is a working paper series published by the Urban Land Institute (ULI) titled *The Ecology of Development: Integrating the Built and Natural Environments*. This publication offers an extraordinarily comprehensive view of sustainable development, termed "ecological development," even encompassing the concept of planning on a human scale. The principal author, ULI member George Brewster, told us that after publication of the first draft in 1996, the project was viewed as too radical and was discontinued by the ULI. Happily, the document has recently found new life and is being published by the California Center for Land Recycling.[18]

Although sustainable development, or green building, is still far from being "business as usual," it is heartening to note that since the completion of Village Homes in 1983, a good deal of progress has been made in the development, refinement, and promotion of these concepts. Some changes have been made in public policy, and actual projects are on the ground. Thus, we are making slow but concrete progress toward practices that are necessary if our society is to sustain itself.

Chapter 7

Location, Size, and Density

The garden city concept was Ebenezer Howard's response a hundred years ago to the problem of overgrowth and congestion of cities and a realization that people wanted to be close to nature. People today are no different. In part, it is that longing to be closer to nature that has driven urban sprawl and the wish for larger and larger individual residential lots.

We agree with the many who believe that large cities have great potential. Designed properly, they can be, and many are today, wonderfully vibrant, culturally rewarding, satisfying places to live—when they have trees, wide sidewalks with benches, beds of flowers, outdoor cafés, and a rich mixture of retail, office, commercial, residential, civic, and cultural uses. The current movement in the United States toward city revitalization reflects the innate appeal of cities and is important from the perspective of maintaining rather than throwing away existing infrastructure and preserving our connection with our culture and history.

However, as the population grows, should every town become a city, continuously becoming more dense and growing at its edges? We think not. We think that Howard was on the right track: after we have taken advantage of the potential for infill development, much of our population growth should be accommodated in largely self-sufficient communities, limited in size and population density but big enough to sustain a variety of industries and to satisfy the everyday wants of the population. Like Howard, we suggest that these towns be surrounded by borders of agricultural land or greenbelts and be connected to one another through a transit system, creating garden cities rather than urban sprawl.

Since Howard's time, the need for such development patterns has become far more pressing, given the alarmingly rapid deterioration of the environment. Because it disperses the population into appropriately sized clusters surrounded by open space, the garden city concept works well in meeting energy needs: photovoltaic panels and solar water heating systems need more access to sunlight than can be found in a city of tall buildings. Air pollutants disperse more readily when they are not concentrated. Natural drainage systems and innovative sewage disposal systems need open space to function. Locally based agriculture needs some room to flourish. Moreover, garden cities have the advantage of paving over less land. They provide room for natural drainage and neighborhood-scale agriculture, and they create more automobile-free places for children to play.

We propose that from an ecological standpoint, much new development should take the form of garden city units, made up of garden village neighborhoods like Village Homes. These garden cities should be located singly or in clusters as appropriate to the site and region.

We should make clear that we do not advocate as the first option the development of multiple new garden cities. Growth needs to occur first through revitalization and redesign of existing neighborhoods, to make them complete by filling in the missing elements of a garden city or garden village. But once a community reaches the point at which new growth begins to create more problems than it solves, usually at a population of about 50,000, it will probably be necessary to establish a location for a new garden city.

Where it is appropriate for growth to take the form of additional sustainable garden cities, some critical planning decisions must be made. In some areas of the country where population growth is occurring very rapidly, these questions are of critical importance:

- Where should new garden cities be located?
- Is there an optimum size for a garden city?
- Is there an optimum population density for a garden city as a whole, for a group of garden cities, or for a whole region?

This is an unusual approach because in planning new development, planners have not traditionally placed much importance on questions of location, size, and density in relationship to sustainability. This is unfortunate. However, the oversight has not been apparent until recently for two main reasons. One is time lag. Patterns of human settlement have changed drastically over the past century. The resulting social and environmental changes have been cumulative and have not been immediately recognized or understood.

The second is technology. Because of advanced technology, society has been able to tell families and businesses, in effect, "Locate wherever you choose. If it happens to be in the desert, we will bring you water—not just enough to drink and bathe in but enough to grow a lawn and roses. If there is not enough space for growing your food and disposing of your wastes, we will bring in your food and carry away your wastes. If the area becomes so crowded that social behavior deteriorates, we will saturate the area with well-equipped police officers to protect you and keep people in line. If you want to live many miles from your job, we will sell you a cheap car and cheap gasoline to burn in it. If the area between your home and your job is already congested with millions of other people and their cars, we will build a freeway to get you through quickly. Whatever problem you encounter can be overcome by technology."

When we think of technology, we tend to think of it as ingenuity, as "American know-how." But technology, and especially today's technology, also includes resources—steel, aluminum, concrete, petroleum and its myriad products, and above all, energy. The amount of energy our technology uses is not immediately apparent because a great deal of it is used indirectly. For example, in shipping food back and forth across the country, the energy used directly is fairly obvious; it powers the truck that transports the food, runs the refrigeration equipment that keeps it fresh, and so on. But making the truck also requires energy—to dig the ore, transport it, refine it into steel, and machine it into parts; to heat or cool the factory and transport the workers to and from their jobs. An economist would say that this energy is "embodied" in the truck. But this is not all; also embodied in the truck is part of the energy required to build the truck plant and produce the materials for the plant; to make the machines that dug the ore, the mills and furnaces that refined it, and the cars that brought the workers to work; to locate and extract the oil and refine the gasoline that the workers' cars used.

A branch of economic statistics called input-output analysis estimates the total amount of any resource embodied directly or indirectly in a particular type of good or service. These figures show that there is a great deal of energy embodied in almost all the goods and services we consume today. Thus, if energy gets scarcer and more expensive, everything gets more scarce and more expensive. Even recycling and renewable resources get more expensive because they, too, require energy. We can already see this happening in our economy, and it is only beginning. As we move away from fossil fuels to avoid the catastrophic effect of carbon dioxide buildup in the atmosphere, many of the new forms of renewable energy will be more expensive than fossil fuels. It seems important to design more efficiently to offset those costs.

This is why there are some right and wrong answers to questions of city location, size, and density. It seems clear that some locations, sizes, and densities require more physical technology to make them work than do others— more nonrenewable resources and more energy. So far, planners have pretty much ignored this fact. However, as resources and energy become more scarce and more expensive, it will become harder and harder to ignore their costs. To maintain current standards of living, energy, water, and nonrenewable resources will have to be used more and more frugally and planners will be led more and more toward locations, sizes, and densities that require the least energy and resources to make them work. They will also be led toward certain ways of laying out cities and villages, new ways of organizing production, and more appropriate lifestyles.

We believe that all these forces may tend to lead us in the same general direction. In this chapter and the following ones, we describe what we think that direction will be. It will not be backward but sideways, toward the kind of society our science and ingenuity might have produced if energy and resources had been scarce all along and if we had better understood the social and ecological consequences of the changes we were making.

Location

Over the past century, locations of new development have been determined almost completely by politics and short-term economics, with little consideration for long-term planning or ecological implications. There have been some exceptions. Construction on floodplains has decreased, though certainly not ceased entirely. Sometimes open space has been preserved for its own sake—if it has some special quality—and some communities have avoided building on agricultural land. To date, however, little of this has had much effect on growth patterns, except in reducing leapfrog development, because the most immediately desirable location for the next bit of development is always on the outskirts of an existing town, convenient to existing services and activities. The political and economic power of landowners on the outskirts, who stand to make huge speculative gains if their land is developed, also supports concentric growth. If there happens to be nothing but prime agricultural land on the outskirts, planners will talk gravely about the undesirability of building there, but in the end, development will proceed. Many times, more serious concerns such as air quality and availability of water are not even addressed.

Thus, planning for garden cities and redevelopment of existing cities into groupings of garden villages goes hand in hand with restricting the concentric growth of existing cities. Fortunately, a willingness seems to be emerging, especially in towns and cities of moderate size, to restrict growth on the peripheries. Petaluma, California, where the issue of growth restrictions was unsuccessfully contested in court in the 1970s, was the first city in California to do so. Since then, fifteen communities in the San Francisco Bay Area alone have adopted urban growth boundaries, primarily through voter initiatives. The American Farmland Trust reported that across the country, there were 10 statewide land protection initiatives, 22 county initiatives, and 93 local initiatives on the November 1998 ballot. Eighty-seven percent of these initiatives passed.[1]

Where further growth is desirable and there is no capacity to absorb infill, new garden cities located adjacent to an existing city might better substitute for sprawling concentric growth. There should be a greenbelt of open space around each new garden city to give it a distinct identity and keep overall regional densities lower. The greenbelt need not be extremely wide so long as there is an effective mechanism to keep it from being destroyed as growth pressures increase. When Michael served on the Davis City Council, it was written into the general plan that after build-out of the plan, at a population of 76,000, which was already becoming less than ideal for a walkable, bikeable community, growth in Davis should occur as infill development or as a compact new town or self-contained district, separated from Davis by a permanent agricultural greenbelt.

In the future, in areas of high population growth it may be necessary to locate much of the new development away from existing urban areas in loca-

Krems, a village in Austria, settles beautifully into the landscape.

tions that provide more of the attributes necessary to sustain a population in ecologically sound ways. This could lead to clusters of revitalized towns or linear strings of new garden cities in what are now rural areas. This can be done without destroying the rural setting if the towns are sited in the way many European towns and villages are—small and with definite boundaries.

Locating sites for these new garden cities will be a difficult job. There are no perfect sites for new towns; some sites are merely preferable to others. There are three important factors to consider:

- Availability of water without nonsustainable demands on groundwater
- Potential for local production of a variety of wholesome foods
- Potential for meeting energy needs locally

Without these, it is impossible to talk of sustainable design in any meaningful sense. They are critical to creating an energy-efficient design. Transporting water and food to areas where they cannot be produced requires tremendous amounts of energy and resources. The same is true of transporting energy, though this is not immediately obvious because we are used to the idea of transmitting electricity for great distances via high-voltage lines. But to do this, some other form of energy must first be converted into electricity, a process that is generally inefficient and very wasteful compared with using the energy where it is produced and in its original form—heat, for example. Even when electricity is generated directly from wind or at a hydroelectric facility, the farther it must travel, the more is lost as a result of resistance in the transmission lines.

Here are some other important ecological and social factors to be considered in selecting a site:

- An absence of high levels of air pollution and radioactivity; climatic conditions that will sufficiently dissipate additional air pollutants produced by the garden city
- Proximity to existing transportation corridors, primarily railroads and also waterways and highways
- Low risk from natural hazards such as earthquakes and floods
- Proximity to a major cultural center
- Scenic beauty, quietness, and pleasant climate

There are few real-life examples of communities that have decided in advance where they want to grow and then have followed through with their plan. Vancouver, British Columbia, is one. Back in the 1960s, when U.S. cities were busy building freeways to enable ever-increasing sprawl, the greater Vancouver area took a different path. With a great deal of citizen input, leaders of the Greater Vancouver Regional District (a regional planning agency with land use powers, made up of twenty-one jurisdictions) decided that the district would accommodate population growth in six new, compact business centers that would serve as multimodal transportation hubs. They created a balance of jobs and housing in each region. They decided that public transit rather than freeways would serve as the primary transportation option, and they designated "green zones" for agriculture and open space. This strategy was successfully carried out.[2]

Today, it is important for planners to take advantage of the rapidly evolving technology of geographic information systems (GIS) mapping, which is making possible very sophisticated decisions regarding where to locate new growth and where to avoid such growth. An example can be found in California's Sierra Nevada mountain range. The Placer County Board of Supervisors, in cooperation with the Sierra Business Council, has initiated a project to map all the sensitive lands in the county in order to determine which sites need to be preserved. Criteria to be considered include open space for recreation, community edges, fire protection, endangered species, agricultural land, and floodplains. Overlay maps of these areas will help local officials identify appropriate sites to preserve and appropriate sites for new development.[3]

Village Homes passes most of the criteria for appropriate location. Northern California's Mediterranean climate allows for natural cooling and solar heating during all but the foggy season, about two to three months of the year. The city of Davis is not on a floodplain and is removed enough from fault lines that the community has never experienced any earthquake damage. Davis sits adjacent to a major highway and is on a rail corridor that runs between Sacramento and San Francisco, our major cultural centers. As the freeways become more crowded, use of the train is increasing.

The Village Homes neighborhood is located on an infill site, sandwiched between two existing developments and across the street from the campus of the University of California, the city's largest employer. It is within walking distance of a neighborhood shopping center. Our neighborhood bicycle system is connected to an extensive network of bicycle paths leading to schools, a shopping center, the town center, the university, and other destinations.

Although the location of Village Homes is a good one because it was an infill site, it is less than ideal because it sits on some of the best agricultural soil one can find. However, we have made good use of this precious resource and calculate that between the vegetable gardens, the fruit trees, and the grapes we grow on overhangs, at least 50 percent of the land is still in cultivation.

Village Homes residents, like people in the rest of Davis, draw their water from underground aquifers. As the city grows, we must be concerned about depleting this resource. Fortunately, in the twenty years that Village Homes has existed, the level of the aquifer has not decreased.

Size and Density

Since the development of the automobile, urban sprawl has become the dominant pattern of development in the United States. It has created vast cities and megacities of uniform medium density, which have neither the advantages of a true compact city nor those of the countryside.

As a society, we were well on our way to destroying our landscape back in 1960, when Lewis Mumford complained about land use patterns in the United States:

> "Park" now usually means a desert of asphalt, designed as a temporary storage space for motorcars; while "field" means another kind of artificial desert, a barren area planted in great concrete strips, vibrating with noise, dedicated to the arrival and departure of planes. From park and field unroll wide ribbons of concrete that seek to increase the speed of travel between distant points at whatever sacrifice of esthetic pleasures or social opportunities. And if our present system of development goes on, without a profound change in our present planning concept and values, the final result will be a universal wasteland, unfit for human habitat, no better than the surface of the moon. No wonder people play with projects for exploring outer space; we have been turning the landscape around our great cities into mere launching platforms, and our long daily journeys in the cramped interiors of motorcars are preparatory trips for the even more cramped and comatose journeys by rocket.[4]

Alas, since the time of Mumford's eloquent observation, the trend has continued and worsened. Since 1970, expansion of the developed area around Chicago has outpaced population growth by a factor of ten. During this same period in Los Angeles, land coverage increased by 200 percent while the population increased by 45 percent.[5] It is not additional parks or larger yards that accounts for the increased space we use per person today— it is the wide ribbons of concrete criticized by Mumford. Half of the urban area of Los Angeles is now devoted to roadways.

A much more appealing and efficient land use pattern, and the one we should work toward, is one of small, relatively dense, complete garden cities with distance between them to reduce regional density. Higher density within the garden city has the advantage of providing stimulating social contact and eliminating most of the need for automobiles by making public transit, bicycling, and walking viable means of transportation. Low overall regional density (achieved by having open space surrounding the garden cities) reduces air pollution, allows local agricultural production for each city's needs, permits easier waste management and recycling, and puts the countryside within easy walking distance of every home. This is essential if we are to live within the limits of renewable energy supplies, maintain a healthy environment, and ensure sustainable food production. To observe what this pattern looks like, one can visit Denmark, the Netherlands, parts of Italy and France, and much of England and Germany, to name a few places. These settlements were originally developed during a time when communities had to be sustainable to survive.

The importance of the density of regions or bioregions as well as that of individual communities is addressed by the concept of carrying capacity. According to Lamont Hempel of Claremont Graduate University in California, multiple factors affect the carrying capacity of a region, including soil, water, food, climate, nutrients, energy supply, natural disasters, and forests. Regional carrying capacity also varies widely over time and space. For

Agricultural land surrounds Bonnieux, a sustainable French village.

Homes in Bonnieux have private gardens.

example, a large estuary can serve as an effective sewage treatment plant as long as the human population nearby is relatively small. If the population grows too much, the estuary's assimilative capacity will be overwhelmed.[6]

Professor Richard T. T. Forman of the Graduate School of Design at Harvard University agrees that considerations of sustainability must be based on a regional perspective:

> Only one approach appears possible concurrently to maintain ecological integrity and basic human needs for the built environment. That is to plan and manage the urban landscape as only one of several linked landscapes considered together. The group as a whole could theoretically be sustainable. Because of the massive inputs and outputs involved, the overwhelming focus of planning and management will have to be on the non-urban landscapes to maintain their ecological integrity, and prevent land degradation. In an era of growing city numbers and sizes, this is a non-trivial step to take.[7]

It is difficult to determine the ideal population size of a community within a region. From an economic standpoint, communities need to be large enough to support the retail services that meet the residents' daily needs. The League of California Cities holds that 7,000 to 8,000 is the minimum population necessary to support adequate municipal services and necessary commercial development. In rural areas, the minimum could be 4,000 to 7,000 people. This is because school districts in rural areas do not object to smaller schools, and small grocery stores may not be competing with larger stores that offer a greater selection and lower prices.

A town with a larger population can support a greater variety of commercial services and job opportunities and might be able to provide some city services (both utilities and social services) at a lower cost per person. A smaller population, on the other hand, gives the town as a whole a stronger sense of community and allows each resident a greater voice in government. Since a garden city's land area would be limited by the need to keep everything within easy walking and bicycling distance (one to four square miles), a smaller population would mean less crowding, which would make it easier to generate enough energy, recycle wastes, and disperse air pollution. On these grounds, we think that 20,000 to 30,000 would be the maximum ideal population for a new garden city of this pattern. It is interesting to note that Ebenezer Howard projected 30,000 as ideal for garden cities in England.[8] By current standards, this is also the size above which it becomes difficult for a city to have only one high school, which in itself has significance because it does not bifurcate the community.

It is interesting to note that a study conducted by Fannie Mae, the nation's largest home-mortgage lender, revealed that more than half of all Americans prefer to live in a small to medium-sized city, a suburb, or a small town and about one in five prefer the rural life. Fewer than one in ten said they prefer to live in a large city.[9]

From an ecological perspective, the physical size of a garden city is as important as the population size. If its radius is less than one mile, walking and bicycling are extremely convenient and can be the major means of transportation. A town with a one-mile radius would be roughly three square miles in area. Let us see what this implies in terms of density. For example, assuming an average of 2.7 people per housing unit, a town with an area of three square miles and a population of 20,000 would have an overall density of about 3.9 units per acre. If residential development takes about half of the land, a residential neighborhood would have a maximum average density of 8 units per acre. This is enough to support a bus system with frequent service and, under the right regional circumstances, a light-rail connection.

A residential density of 7 to 8 units per acre is rather high compared with present development standards, but it does not represent overcrowding for several reasons. First, deemphasizing the automobile can save a great deal of space that is otherwise devoted to streets and parking. Second, the sense of overcrowding depends largely on design as well as density, and during the reign of the automobile, we have lost much of our sense of how to design comfortable compact housing. We can make a great deal of improvement merely by relearning traditional design solutions used before the automobile, such as the court-garden style of house that appears in various forms all over the world, in a wide range of climates and cultures. Most traditional towns throughout Europe offer excellent examples.

Some planning critics today believe that the densities proposed here are far too low. They favor extremely high urban density, achieved mainly by use of multi-unit structures and elimination of private yards. The extreme of this school of thought is represented by the massive, multistoried single-structure cities proposed by architect Paolo Soleri. Proponents of very high urban density generally believe that it is necessary in order to conserve agricultural land and preserve areas of wilderness and sparsely populated countryside. They also argue that multi-unit dwellings save building materials and that they conserve energy by minimizing heat loss through exterior walls.

That they require somewhat less building material is true, but their energy savings are probably very small if they are located in large urban areas. Any energy savings in multi-unit buildings may well be offset by the energy required to transport food into a densely populated area and transport waste out of it. Air pollution and noise also become more concentrated in densely populated areas.

We have noticed that we consume less energy at home in Davis than we do when we visit Los Angeles or San Francisco. In Davis, when the weather is warm, we open the windows at night, but in the city, we succumb to keeping windows closed and turning on the air conditioner so that we are not kept awake by the noise and automobile exhaust from outside.

The ideal urban density is high enough to allow residents to walk, bike, or take transit to work, school, and other destinations but low enough to allow most of the needed energy to be produced on or near the site, as well as most of the food. Ideal densities will allow waste to be recycled on or near the site and provide enough space to disperse smoke and other air pollutants. In effect, the ideal density is that which does not exceed the carrying capacity of the area.

Conservation of agricultural land is a stronger argument for high urban densities, but it is not as strong as it may at first appear. If population growth must occur in locations where only good agricultural land is available for development, a high population density may be justified. But it would be more to the point to ask why population growth should take place in such locations at all. Because we are used to urbanization and concentric growth, we tend to assume that growth must take place around existing population centers and that we have little choice in the matter. But with self-contained garden cities and villages, we do have a choice. Even the richest farming areas contain sites with lower agricultural value. These same sites often have special aesthetic appeal. Sites located away from flat agricultural lands often have not been used because they are slightly more expensive to build on and require more imaginative planning. But if we are seriously interested in preserving agricultural land, these are the sites we should be developing.

On a rocky or hilly site, development can actually increase agricultural productivity simply because of the detailed attention the home gardener is willing to give to terracing, erosion control, and soil improvement. In many cases, homeowners can produce food on land that would normally be rejected for farming.

As mentioned previously, the average density of an entire region may be as important a measure of appropriateness as the density within those areas of the region that are developed. High-density living in Vancouver, British Columbia, for instance, is made enjoyable by the recreational open space maintained within the city in the form of trails, beaches, and parks. There is also magnificent visual open space because the city is located on beautiful waterways and within view of majestic mountains. Through good regional planning, adjacent agricultural areas are also being preserved.

The major objection to very high population densities, however, is simply that they can create a less than optimal or even oppressive living environment. Surely we have learned this from the results of housing projects built in the 1960s where large numbers of low-income people were packed into multistoried buildings. Taxpayers are now paying the cost of those mistakes as these buildings are torn down and remodeled into lower-density developments. It is unfortunate that urban planners of the 1960s failed to heed the conclusions of the experts of earlier decades.

Lewis Mumford reported that members of the Regional Planning Association of America learned from the mistakes of their predecessors that projects of very high density carry serious costs: "The increased burden on nonexistent parks, playgrounds, schools, the excessive costs of traffic congestion and avenue widening in cities developed now for five or six times their original density—heavily outweighs all the visible economies."[10] These planners were responding to the enormous problems that existed in cities of more than 100 persons per acre.

High population density has its most obvious effects on the poorest and least mobile individuals living in the inner cities, but the effects also reach

High-density housing developments such as this one in Glendale, California, often poorly designed, have gotten a bad name in many communities. (Photograph courtesy of the city of Glendale)

the upper economic levels. The more affluent tend to lose their sensitivity to the value of life and their capacity for helping and caring about others. They are forced to suppress their natural compassion for the less fortunate individuals they see all around them because their problems are so overwhelming or because fears for their own safety prevent them from becoming directly involved.

Human lives tend to be impoverished by a lack of private or semiprivate open space. Public open spaces and natural areas within a city are better than none at all, of course. But if we assume that humans are most at home in a natural environment because that is the setting in which we evolved, it follows that each of us needs a bit of nature at home: a piece of earth where we can enjoy sun, wind, rain, and growing things in privacy and where we can fully interact with nature—not merely observe and experience but dig, plant, prune, and harvest. This is especially true for the majority of us who do not work on the land for our living.

The social and psychological benefits provided by green space have been well documented. Research indicates that views of vegetation and nature help people relax and concentrate. One study revealed that hospitalized patients who had views of nature and spent time outdoors needed less medication, slept better, and were happier than patients without these connections to nature.[11] Other research shows that humans derive substantial pleasure from trees, whether it be feelings of relaxation, connection to nature, or religious joy.[12]

Public green spaces between multistoried housing complexes are no substitute for private, semiprivate, or cooperative yards, however. Architect Oscar Newman, in his study of housing projects in New York City, documented that robberies were two and one-half times as frequent in fourteen-story high-rise public housing projects surrounded by public open space as in three- to six-story walk-up buildings constructed around semiprivate courtyards. The two types of housing project in Newman's study contained the same number of residents, were built at the same density, and were located across the street from each other. The differences arose in the height of the buildings and the percentage of ground-level space they occupied. The low-rise buildings covered 23 percent of the available land, whereas the high-rise buildings occupied only 16.6 percent of the total area. Residents of the low-rise buildings were able to develop a sense of ownership of their space and a sense of community, but those living in the high-rise buildings had to fend for themselves and were not very successful at doing so.[13]

Not only do people seem to need their own piece of ground; we also seem to want to be able to experience larger expanses of open space. It is significant that people seeking a high state of awareness or a high spiritual level have traditionally gravitated to natural settings with limited populations, such as mountains or deserts. Many of us have personally experienced the soothing effect of retreating into the countryside or wilderness. Social scientists H. H. Iltes, P. Andrews, and O. L. Loucks stated:

> Unique as we may think we are, we are nevertheless as likely to be genetically programmed to a natural habitat of clean air and varied green landscape as any other mammal. To be relaxed and feel healthy usually means simply allowing our bodies to react in the way which one hundred millions of years of evolution has equipped us. Physically and genetically, we appear best adapted to a tropical savanna, but as a cultural animal we utilize learned adaptations to cities and towns. For thousands of years we have tried in our houses to imitate not only the climate, but also the setting of our evolutionary past: warm, humid air, green plants, and even animal companions. Today, if we can afford it, we may even build a greenhouse or swimming pool next to our living room, buy a place in the country, or at least take our children vacationing on the seashore. The specific physiological reactions to natural beauty and diversity, to the shapes and colors of nature (especially to green), to the motions and sounds of other animals, such as birds, we as yet do not comprehend. But it is evident that

nature in our daily life should be thought of as a part of the biological need. It cannot be neglected in the discussions of resource policy for man.[14]

It is not surprising, then, that when the *Wall Street Journal* surveyed home buyers to find out what amenities they wanted most, natural open space was at the top of the list—77 percent of those polled said they thought it was "extremely important."[15] Further, studies show that homes located near a greenbelt or open space sell for more than neighboring homes that are not on the greenbelt. A study conducted in Boulder, Colorado, revealed the aggregate property value of a neighborhood with a greenbelt to be about $5.4 million more than if there had been no greenbelt.[16]

It should be noted as a footnote to this section that although local governments do have the legal authority to determine the size and density of new developments and the densities of infill projects and redevelopment projects, the current legal and political constraints on limiting the population size of cities as a whole are enormous. We found through our experience as citizen activists in Davis that although we can slow growth, the legal system does not allow us to stop it. After densifying, Davis's only alternative to sprawl is to locate new population growth in an adjacent but separate site.

The small city of Carmel, California, succeeded in stopping growth by establishing growth boundaries and limiting water supplies. Santa Barbara County also limited water availability as a strategy for limiting population growth. County supervisors voted to turn down an opportunity to tie into a state water project. However, in a subsequent drought, the county supervisors who had supported this strategy were caught in an angry public backlash when residents suddenly were unable to water their lawns and their previously lush, green landscapes turned brown.

Coastal communities of California and also, to some extent, the city of Davis have seen population growth slowed somewhat by higher housing prices because they are more desirable places to live. Certainly this factor has also helped stop growth in Carmel. There is, of course, an equity problem with slowing or stopping growth in this way. To some extent, Davis has addressed this situation through extremely aggressive affordable housing programs, but truly fair and effective political and legal mechanisms for limiting the size of cities are, unfortunately, not yet in place.

Critics of the ideas about density and crowding presented here may argue that our conclusions are highly speculative. Admittedly, they are. Nevertheless, urban designers and policy makers are required to make decisions every day regarding density, size or availability of private yards, and access to open space. Until there is evidence to the contrary, it seems wisest to proceed on the following two assumptions: (1) there are limits on the environmental conditions to which humans can adapt, and (2) the kind of environment we evolved in is the best guide to what we are physically and socially comfortable with and consistently most healthy living in.

The size of Village Homes—sixty acres—puts it in the category of a small neighborhood that depends on the surrounding community for most of its jobs, retail services, and schools. A sustainable community or garden city would be made up of a collection of neighborhoods the size of Village Homes.

The density of Village Homes was determined in advance through the master plan, which provides for 242 housing units. If the acreage devoted to open space and agriculture is subtracted, the density is about 7 units per acre. At the time we were building the development, this was somewhat more dense than the standard, and we were warned by real estate agents that our houses were placed too close together. However, because every home looks out on open space—a common-area greenbelt or agricultural land—and there are no fences in the heavily vegetated common areas, the community has the atmosphere of a rural landscape.

The community's overall density, including agricultural land and open space, is just 4 units per acre. We were warned at the time that even this was too high, but if we were designing the project by today's standards, we would build a higher-density development with more common-wall homes and more small apartment units. Demand for the apartment units, including the one-bedroom units located above the Village Homes offices, has been extraordinary. We would like to add a gardener's cottage to the western end of the development near the playground and row crops. There has been some vandalism there at night that would be halted if there were windows overlooking the area. However, any proposed increase in the density of the development has met with angry opposition from a small but extremely vocal group of residents. We have discovered that the time to increase density was when we were building the development. Any changes proposed now encounter fear and opposition from some residents.

The Village Homes experience has taught us that it is possible to create a semirural environment in which residents are physically and socially comfortable and healthy at an overall density (including parks and agricultural lands) of 4 units per acre. We have yet to hear a single complaint that our residents feel crowded.

Lest we become too satisfied with the accomplishments of Village Homes, however, we need only look at the work of educators and planners

William Rees and Mathis Wackernagel addressing the concept of the ecological footprint to realize that there is much more to do. The ecological footprint is an indicator of the combined ecological effects of per capita consumption and population growth. It measures how much of nature's carrying capacity we use to feed, house, and otherwise maintain ourselves. Footprint analysis starts with the observation that all consumption of energy and materials and all discharge of wastes requires a finite amount of land or water area for resource production and waste disposal.

This area can actually be estimated for a country, a community, or an individual household using information about how much food, energy, water, and other resources are used by a given population and how much of that is turned into waste that ends up on land or in the water. Although we do not have ecological footprints for the people living in Village Homes, we do know that in the United States, the average ecological footprint is twenty-five acres per person, as compared with Bangladesh, where it is one acre per person. The collective footprint of the 9.5 million people of sprawling Los Angeles County is at least forty times larger than the county itself and, in fact, larger than the entire land area of California.[17] Thus, in terms of long-term sustainability, we in the West have much work to do in modifying our commuting habits, changing our lifestyles, improving technology, and changing the methods and politics of land use planning.

Chapter 8

Designing with Nature for People: A Sustainable Approach to Urban Design

Previous chapters have documented society's past failure to take the environment into consideration when building communities. The results bear repeating: polluted water and air, agricultural land and animal habitat paved over by development, and a dependence on nonrenewable forms of energy and other resources. However, there are ways to accommodate the human population in communities that both preserve the natural environment and better meet people's physical and social needs.

The key to sustainable development lies in having planners and engineers understand and work with nature and human nature rather than habitually trying to overcome them. Experience shows that collaboration with nature is less costly and more effective in the long run. In this chapter, we suggest some comprehensive urban design elements of communities designed with nature for people. Based in part on our experience with Village Homes, they integrate into an urban form the considerations that are important to sustainability and the human spirit. First, we consider the garden city as a more sustainable urban form of development and examine its basic building blocks: garden village neighborhoods and town centers. Next, we look at circulation systems. Finally, we address landscaping and drainage.

Urban Form: Revisiting the Garden City

As discussed throughout this book, we advocate a modular rather than a piecemeal approach to planning based on the garden city model. Again, a garden city is not equivalent to a legally incorporated city; rather, it is a planning unit that can either stand on its own or be a part of a larger city or urban area.

135

The two most important features of the garden city pattern are (1) heavy emphasis on pedestrian and bicycle traffic and (2) a high degree of self-reliance. As noted in chapter 7, both of these have important implications for size. The garden city must be small enough that distances are suitable for walking and bicycling, but at the same time it must be large enough to satisfy most of its residents' needs within the community, providing food, energy, and a variety of jobs, housing, goods and services, and recreational and social opportunities. These two requirements set fairly definite upper and lower limits on the size and density of an appropriately designed garden city or village. It should not be larger in area than about four square miles, and if it is to support regional light-rail transit, it needs to be quite compact, particularly in the town center. A site larger than this requires two garden cities, each one separate and complete in itself, even though the two may be adjacent.

A garden city should be made up of garden village neighborhoods—each large enough to provide some commercial and professional services—surrounding a town center. The garden city should have the following features:

- A core area offering a wide range of goods and services and a public transit stop located within one and one-fourth to one and one-half miles of all residents
- A concentration of higher-density housing within one-half mile of the core area
- An internal circulation pattern emphasizing and giving direct access to pedestrian and bicycle traffic and minimizing human contact with automobile traffic
- Land set aside for agricultural use
- Provision for commercial and industrial enterprises that would provide work for a high proportion of residents
- A mix of housing types that includes affordable housing for all income groups
- A full range of primary and secondary schools
- A full range of recreational opportunities
- Street design and general planning to minimize costs and energy demands for construction and maintenance of roads, sewers, and the like
- Use of locally available renewable energy sources and energy conservation measures to make the garden city as nearly energy self-sufficient as possible

- Ecologically sound patterns of agriculture, waste management, and resource use (including water use)

This list of features is not intended to be final or exhaustive, and not every garden city will achieve all of them with great success. Not every element of the theoretically ideal town will be possible or appropriate in every garden city. The basic point is simply that designation of a garden city should be a clear statement of general planning intent to make development address the whole range of planning problems humanity faces and to do whatever is possible to solve them.

Garden Village Neighborhoods

The garden village neighborhood is a vital component of the garden city. Unfortunately, the neighborhood has gone almost totally unrecognized as an important element in the design of urban environments. This is surprising because the neighborhood should be as meaningful a social unit as are the individual home and the city. The neighborhood should provide for a certain set of functions, and the diverse elements of the neighborhood should be put together in such a way as to accommodate those functions. Just as a home is designed with certain rooms where family members can go to be alone and other rooms that accommodate group activities, so should the neighborhood be designed to offer opportunities for both privacy and community.

Just as we have strongly advocated specific, well-defined garden city units, we advocate well-defined and comprehensively designed neighborhoods within those cities. A good neighborhood will offer security and privacy and will enhance residents' feelings of identity yet satisfy their needs for diversity and a sense of community. The neighborhood can be merely a site where houses are located, with very little interaction among households, or it can be a more cohesive unit in which a great deal of interaction takes place. It can be a social living environment similar to the villages, tribes, and living groups that humans have been part of for thousands of years. It can be the kind of living environment for which we are genetically adapted—one that allows us the opportunity to more easily satisfy our basic social needs of identity, security, and community and that gives us the social experiences that help us learn to better relate to other individuals.

It seems clear that in comparison with primitive societies, modern society is lacking in quality of human relationships, primarily because it is structured so that people can get along without much communication or cooperation. This is obvious in suburbs, where each household owns a separate lot surrounded by a fence, and all public facilities, shops, restaurants, offices, theaters, and schools are in another part of the town, so there is no spontaneous contact with anyone in the neighborhood.

In such settings, people tend to find human contact in substitute activities: through lodges and country clubs, churches, and popular causes. Some people do fairly well this way, but most of us do not realize how much time and effort goes into creating the interaction that only a few decades ago arose naturally from the things people did in groups to satisfy basic material needs. Rather than meeting our neighbors while walking our dog in the neighborhood park, we must make an appointment to have dinner. Because today's contrived interaction is not essential to the people involved, it has a different quality, and because it takes more time, we tend to do it less.

The importance of making our neighborhoods conducive to a spirit of cooperation and mutual support, rather than one of isolation and mutual distrust, cannot be overemphasized. Our state of mind and even our physical health are profoundly affected by the social climate of our neighborhood environments.

Consider the example of Roseto, a borough in Pennsylvania. Until very recently, Roseto was a small, close-knit Italian American community based on Old World cultural patterns. The community coped with crises and problems as a whole, providing a great deal of emotional security to its members. A study completed in 1978 by the University of Oklahoma found that the people in Roseto had a remarkably low death rate, especially from heart attack, and that very few of them suffered from emotionally related illnesses.

In recent times, Roseto has grown from a close-knit village into a typical suburban town "complete with Cadillacs, swimming pools, country clubs, and heart attacks." Researchers now say that the sources of social and emotional security are being lost and so is the unusually good health of the residents.[1]

Undoubtedly, there are elements that are essential to a community in order for it to continue to function well over time. The following sections examine elements that appear to be needed in the support of an ongoing, well-functioning neighborhood community: appropriate scale, clear boundaries, commonly held land, reliable sources of revenue, security and safety, privacy, and diversity.

APPROPRIATE SCALE

Just as large and small towns have both advantages and disadvantages, so do large and small neighborhoods. In a very small neighborhood, there is not as much diversity, but it is easier to know all the people well. Larger neighborhoods offer more diversity and can become stronger economically, but as they get bigger, they lose the feeling of community.

Author Kirkpatrick Sale, in his book *Human Scale*, presents a number of arguments indicating that 500 people is an optimum number for a neighborhood community in order to have social harmony:

> Anthropology and history both suggest, as we have seen, that humans have been able to work out most of their differences at the population levels clustering around the "magic numbers" of 500–1,000 and 5,000–10,000.
>
> For the first, John Pfeiffer notes that anthropological literature indicates that it is when a population reaches about 1,000 that "a village begins to need policing," and as we have seen, the Dinka villages, like villages in most stateless societies, hold about 500 people on average and almost never more than 1,000. (Rough figures for the village sizes in some other stateless societies: 100–1,000 for the Mandavi, 50–400 for the Amba, 300–500 for the Lugbara, 200–300 for the Konkomba, 400–500 for the Tupi.) Evidently in these face-to-face societies, where every person is known to every other—and presumably every idiosyncrasy, sore spot, boiling point, and the final straw—it is comparatively easy to keep the peace and comparatively easy to restore it once broken. Confirmation comes from the New England towns, the great majority of which were under 1,000, where harmony was the regular rule and "concord and consensus" the norm; from the Chinese villages of all periods until the most recent, with rarely more than 500 people, where traditional law of many varying kinds operated independently of dynastic decrees; from Russia, where the traditional *mir*, with seldom more than 600 or 700 people, was the basic peace-keeping unit for more than a millennium, each with its own version of customary law and all without codification or judicial apparatus.[2]

On the basis of our experience of living in Village Homes, we agree that the optimum number is 500 people or about 150 homes. When the neighborhood consisted of fewer than 100 households, there seemed to be a lack of individual diversity and resources, and as the number of households approached 200, it seemed that the residents had more difficulty knowing a significant number of their neighbors. At that point, the sense of community seemed not quite as strong.

A bank of almond trees marks the eastern boundary of Village Homes.

BOUNDARIES

One reason why there is so little sense of community in endless, sprawling, look-alike development is that no one has a sense of being in a neighborhood. Clear boundaries, on the other hand, make it possible for people to know where one neighborhood ends and the next one begins. They allow the neighborhood to be perceived and appreciated as a unit, and this brings about a sense of identity with both home and community. Boundaries can be created with such features as streets, distinctive architectural styles, gates, and greenbelts. Greenbelts and open space seem to be both more obvious and more pleasant boundaries than streets and are vastly superior to fences and locked gates.

COMMONLY HELD LAND

The modern neighborhood has very little to offer in terms of reasons for the residents to get together. Even neighborhoods that have a homeowners' association and share a swimming pool offer little incentive. Decisions such as determining the hours when the pool will be available do not offer enough reason to get involved to the extent that a great deal of community spirit can develop.

Some neighborhoods do rally together when faced with an outside threat, but once the threat is gone, the community spirit may gradually dissipate. For example, a suburban neighborhood where we once lived was threatened with a poorly planned adjacent development. As residents organized to fight the development, some very pleasant side effects occurred. There were neighborhood potlucks, parties, and organized games in the park. Suddenly, everyone seemed to know everyone else and the neighborhood grew warmer and felt safer.

But once the external threat was gone and the neighboring property was satisfactorily developed, the parties, the fun, and the sense of togetherness gradually disappeared. There was no longer a compelling reason to keep us coming together. However, when community members have control over land and common food production, they have the opportunity to develop meaningful social relationships through working together on something worthwhile.

Any number of experiences with community gardens have shown that the gardens are not only good for producing food; they are also good for developing a sense of community. Self-help housing projects also tend to foster group cohesiveness because of the mutual aid required by the building process.

We once visited an older neighborhood in Portland that had a small park situated among the homes. Previously, the area had been overgrown with weeds and was a hangout for drug dealers. However, at some point, the neighbors had decided to take over the property. They cleaned it up and planted roses. The drug dealers went away, and a sense of neighborhood ownership and pride is now there instead.

Because Village Homes is organized into clusters of eight houses that, in addition to their separate lots, share a common area consisting of about one-fifth to one-fourth acre of land, small groups can accomplish even more at the community level, including sharing a common orchard, an outside entertainment area, and spaces for small children to play. While participating as members of both the overall Village Homes community and a common area, we have observed that some people (10 to 20 percent) do not participate at all (yet most of them seem pleased to be part of the neighborhood). Sixty to 80 percent of the people participate in community activities in varying degrees, and another 10 to 20 percent are very active in all areas of the community. Varying levels of participation are to be expected because people's need to interact socially and to participate in or lead groups and activities will vary.

The key point is that in Village Homes, shared property continues to provide places and reasons to get together. Twenty years after construction of the development, there is still a strong sense of commitment to carry on the traditions of a harvest party, Christmas party, and Easter party. In addition, there are several impromptu potluck get-togethers on an almost weekly basis.

We do not advocate in any way the exclusivity that comes with gated communities and their fenced clubhouses and private pools. Community-owned property can be there for the enjoyment of all, as are the Village Homes playing fields, which host young soccer players from all over the city, and our bike paths, which connect with neighborhoods on either side of us.

When towns and cities are broken down into smaller neighborhood communities, many more people who would like to have leadership roles get such an opportunity. And although the degree of interaction stimulated by the Village Homes design does expose the inability of some members of the population to work together in social situations, this can benefit these people by giving them an opportunity for personal growth.

REVENUE

For a neighborhood to be able to carry out common projects, it needs not only land but also revenue. This can come from donations or assessments or from income from a business source. Assessments are the traditional method of raising money in condominium-type projects. They pay for the construction, management, and maintenance of a multitude of different recreational amenities and open space, including pools, craft rooms, and social centers. Assessments are much like taxes, and even though they allow people to have more control over their condominium development, they are not desirable if other sources of revenue can be found. In Village Homes, ongoing revenue from the lease of land and buildings owned by the homeowners' association and from the sale of almonds reduces the financial burden on individuals.

In less fortunate communities, revenue might appropriately come from foundations or social service funds. This is the case with the Mutual Assistance Network of Del Paso Heights, a distressed neighborhood in Sacramento, California. The county and city were pouring enormous amounts of money into the area with very little benefit until a neighborhood-based nonprofit organization was formed that provides far more cost-effective and responsive programs to address the needs of neighborhood residents. This community now has the resources it needs to help itself.

The city of Seattle maintains a Department of Neighborhoods whose mission is to preserve and enhance the city's diverse neighborhoods and empower people to make positive contributions in their communities. The cornerstone of the Seattle effort is a program of matching funds now offering more than $3.5 million per year to neighborhood residents or businesses for neighborhood planning, organizing, and improvement projects. Any group may apply for funding but must provide a 50 percent in-kind contribution or cash match. This requirement has worked to ensure that projects are a joint effort of numerous participants within a neighborhood.

The matching fund program has resulted in exemplary neighborhood improvement projects and partnerships between neighborhoods and schools. Although the city devotes significant resources to these efforts, the cost-effectiveness of this approach to neighborhood revitalization is enormous, providing both social and economic paybacks. Since the program's inception in 1988, more than 1,000 matching fund projects have been completed, and their success has resulted in continuing increases in the amount of general fund monies allocated to this program. The enthusiasm and spirit of the neighborhood residents participating in this effort is infectious.

Where people have resources to manage and improve their neighborhoods, there is a sense of connection and pride that leads to happier, empowered, and more responsible residents and safer neighborhoods. The programs in Sacramento and Seattle eliminate the dismal view of government as a vending machine—put your money in and get the services out—and leads to more responsible, happier citizens and stronger neighborhood communities.

SECURITY AND SAFETY

Security and safety are important elements in every neighborhood, yet many neighborhoods in the United States are becoming increasingly prone to the ravages of burglars, rapists, vandals, and so on. The usual response is to keep the children close to home and to keep guard dogs or install special locks or security systems.

Several researchers, however, have discovered that urban design can have an effect on crime prevention and that neighborhoods following certain layouts are statistically more likely to be safe places to live. In his book *Design Guidelines for Creating Defensible Space,* architect Oscar Newman points out that one cause of crime is the failure of residents to control surrounding open space, where intruders, if unchallenged, can commit criminal acts. Planning decisions regarding public, semipublic, semiprivate, and private spaces can be made that tend to further recognition of neighbors and outsiders and to encourage residents to assert their dominance against unwelcome persons. If a space is clearly designated as private or semiprivate, residents will act to protect it, whereas a "public" space is always seen as "someone else's" responsibility. This is not to say that all public parks are bad, but often they do have to be policed.

Another key to designing crime-free spaces is enabling residents to see what is going on in the open space around individual dwelling units. Newman contends that too many contemporary housing designs fail to provide for surveillance of the space that is crucial for residents' security—the nearby open space.

Newman also comments on street widths, noting that a wide street becomes a public space, ignored by the neighborhood, whereas a narrow street is psychologically assimilated into the neighborhood. In the latter case, residents are more likely to halt a speeding car or admonish a misbehaving pedestrian.[3] Streets in Village Homes are narrow and are dead-end. In this situation, streets become less public and more controlled because the number of persons who may legitimately use them is limited.

The cluster commons in Village Homes are designed using several techniques to ensure that residents can exert control over adjacent open space. Homes have windows and decks for outdoor living that overlook the common space. Residents have planned and maintained their commons, they have a vested interest in the spaces, and they have every right to protect these areas from intruders. Even the more public greenbelts are less vulnerable to vandalism than an adjacent neighborhood park. Residents pay directly for maintenance of the greenbelts; they have played a part in hiring the gardeners; and they may have participated in planning or building a pool, play structure, or orchard. Therefore, they have a direct interest in defending the open spaces around them. The space is perceived of and is Village Homes territory, not public territory.

The design techniques for provision of safety and security described here work equally well in the inner city. An appropriately designed moderate-income housing development in San Francisco called St. Francis Square provides an instructive example.

St. Francis Square is located in the middle of a high-crime area in the city, yet the residents consider it a fairly safe place to live and to raise children. A number of planning elements have contributed to this. First, the 300 units in three-story buildings are grouped around three landscaped interior courts, and all units have a view of this open area. The apartments are arranged so that groups of six units share a common entry, and each unit has a private garden or balcony. In this way, St. Francis Square provides semipublic space (the courtyard), semiprivate space (the entry corridor), and private space (the apartment and garden or balcony). Second, the residents do not rent their apartments; they own them through membership in a cooperative. An active co-op association controls and manages the jointly owned common space. A strong sense of community is apparent in St. Francis Square that results from

At St. Francis Square, a housing co-op in San Francisco, homes overlook courtyards and residents watch out for one another.

membership in the co-op and participation in community-wide social events and work parties. Even though the rates of street crime in the area surrounding St. Francis Square are very high, the majority of residents feel safe walking in the interior courts at night. It has been reported that if a person is attacked at night and calls out for help, the neighbors respond and the culprit is caught or runs away.[4]

A sense of community is another important variable in the safety of a neighborhood. Where neighbors know and care about one another, they will also act to protect their fellow residents from a suspicious stranger. Neighborhood watch programs have been shown to reduce burglaries by as much as 37 percent.[5] Similarly, researchers at Harvard University reported that rates of violent crime in communities in which residents watched out for one another and for their neighborhood were as much as 40 percent lower than in neighborhoods where such relationships were not as strong. Race and income were not factors in neighbors' willingness to get involved. Some affluent neighborhoods had a poor sense of community, and some of the poorest had a strong one. "It's a social phenomenon," said the study's director, Felton Earls, a professor of psychiatry at the Harvard School of Public Health. "It happens when people are in the street, when people are speaking to each other and when there are activities that bring people together. It feeds on itself."[6]

Crime rates in Village Homes are said to be the lowest in the city of Davis. Research indicates that it is apparently not just the delineation of spaces into semipublic and semiprivate areas that allows Village Homes to be relatively free of crime. The things we have done to offer places and reasons for people to come together has created that sense of community that results in good neighbors and a safe environment.

PRIVACY

It is very likely that physical privacy is essential to the development of a sense of community in our culture. It has been observed by anthropologist Edward T. Hall and others that where physical barriers do not provide enough privacy, social barriers develop as substitutes.[7]

In a crowded apartment house with poor sound insulation between the walls, neighbors often make a point of not getting to know one another so that they can maintain distance through social barriers if not through physical design. In her graduate research at the University of California, Judy observed this social withdrawal or "hiding," which gives the harassed individual the privacy he or she so badly needs.

Occasionally, we meet individuals who seem to have relinquished their privacy in favor of a more communal lifestyle. This arrangement rarely lasts very long. Soon, the freshman deserts her crowded dormitory for a quiet apartment off campus or the commune member leaves to find a place of his own. For a lasting community spirit to develop, it seems essential that group members have an opportunity for privacy.

When designing Village Homes, we believed it was necessary to provide plenty of opportunity to satisfy the need for privacy. Every home has space for a fenced, private yard. Sound insulation is installed between common-wall units. Large expanses of windows either are screened or face courtyards or open space. The Homeowner's Association appointed design review committee monitors new construction to ensure that future additions will not detract from any individual's ability to maintain privacy. No second-story window may face another's private yard.

DIVERSITY

In chapter 3, we identified diversity as a necessary component of a well-functioning human settlement; it is just as much a necessary component of a well-functioning neighborhood. Unfortunately, modern neighborhoods have been growing less diverse. Just as we have moved toward large-scale farming exemplified by rows and rows of a single crop, we have moved toward neighborhoods that segregate people of similar social class into endless vertical and horizontal rows of housing units, separated from the shops, workplaces, schools, parks, and civic facilities essential to daily living.

It has been demonstrated that children suffer from neighborhood homogeneity. A study in West Germany compared the reactions of children living in eighteen new communities with those of youngsters living in older, more diverse German cities. The children in the new communities did not like their living environments very much. According to the *New York Times,* in the new towns, "amid soaring rectangular shapes of apartment houses with shaded walks, big lawns, and fenced-in play areas, the children for whom much of this has been designed apparently feel isolated, regimented and bored."[8]

To maintain an appropriate level of diversity, neighborhoods should incorporate the following:

- Housing for people of various income levels
- Space for field games
- Natural play areas
- A large party or meeting facility
- Spaces for informal gatherings, such as a well-placed bench under an appealing tree
- Recreational facilities such as a swimming pool, a basketball court, and an arts and crafts center
- Agricultural production
- A small commercial center including a neighborhood store, a restaurant, and small shops and offices

Although all these items need not be included in every neighborhood, designers would do well to remember that a more diverse neighborhood will be more full of vitality.

A neighborhood functions well when people feel that they are safe and can rely on help from others. It functions well when people can grow in their ability to get along and work out their differences. It functions well when, through participation in community activities, including work and fun in groups, people experience the inner warmth and fullness that come from feeling that they as individuals are part of the community and that the community as a whole is part of all humanity. All neighborhoods should be designed to accommodate these functions, for when they are not, part of the human potential may be lost.

Neighborhoods can also play an important role in creating a participatory democracy. Mark Hatfield, former U.S. senator from Oregon, said:

> We must return to a scale of government which is comprehensive to our citizens. . . . To date, the centralization of government has destroyed community self management and citizen participation. We must reverse this trend and develop our cities along the lines of neighborhood government and inter-neighborhood cooperation.[9]

The Town Center

The town center has the potential of being a friendly and exciting place for the people who work, shop, find entertainment, or reside there. It ties a group of neighborhoods together and provides an environment of diverse activities that contrasts with the outlying neighborhoods.

Most towns and cities in the United States have lost most, if not all, of the essence of the town center as it existed in many places in the middle of the twentieth century. With sprawling growth, people are moving farther and farther from the town center. Peripheral shopping centers have sprung up away from town centers, reducing the economic viability of businesses in the town's core. People visit their town center less frequently, thereby reducing their feeling of belonging to the town.

The shopping center serves as a place to purchase goods and services, but for the most part, it fails to function as a town center for the area it serves. This is partly because as the name implies, the shopping center is just for shopping; it lacks the range of activities and facilities found in a real town center. It is not a workplace, except for the shop personnel, nor a center of local government; nobody actually lives there, and there are no schools or public recreation areas. Aside from a few restaurants, there is little or no space for leisure or socializing. There are no plazas or civic spaces.

The shopping center also fails to function as a town center because it is oriented to automobiles. Acres of surrounding land, in a prime location for needed nonshopping facilities, are taken up by parking lots. Even where other facilities exist nearby, they are typically separated by busy streets and long stretches of barren parking lots, quite inhospitable to pedestrians.

To function well as a town center, an area should have shops, businesses, restaurants, sidewalk cafés, theaters, schools, compact housing, a transit stop, and professional and governmental offices. It should also have open spaces in the form of parks, plazas, bowling greens, and so on. It must also be very compact, without large parking lots, blank walls, or vacant parcels interrupting the flow. With this variety of elements, it can be an exciting and vibrant place to be, to live, and to meet people, as well as a place to shop and do business.

As far back as 1953, Lewis Mumford wrote:

> Above everything else, a city is a means of providing a maximum number of social contacts and satisfactions. When the open spaces gape too widely, and dispersal is too constant, the people lack a stage for their activities and the drama of their daily life lacks sharp focus. Like every other amenity, public open spaces and private gardens must be scaled to the whole for which they are planned.[10]

This vision of the town center depends partly on good design, partly on a lively diversity of activities, and partly on size. Also very important is the absence of speeding automobiles. Eliminating or reducing the size of automobile traffic lanes as well as large surface parking lots will make the area more compact and thus easier to get around in on foot with no need to be alert for cars. Undistracted by their noise, motion, and brightness, strolling pedestrians will be better able to appreciate the sights, sounds, and smells of human activity. The air will be cleaner, and the atmosphere of the street will

Downtown Santa Monica, California, has eliminated automobiles, but the lively, mixed-use area attracts thousands of visitors. (Photograph courtesy of Local Government Commission)

be calmer and quieter, more conducive to browsing, to striking up a conversation, or to settling down on a bench to rest and just observe.

The town center seems to function better if it has its own neighborhood community. People can live there in flats above businesses, in small apartments, and in town houses. These alternatives offer a perfect situation for people who want to live in an area of higher density. Senior citizens who may no longer drive and young unmarried individuals are particularly drawn to downtown living. A few merchants or craftspeople may even combine their places of business and their living quarters. This sort of mixed use adds to the liveliness and homeyness of the downtown area and makes it a safer place because people are present at all times of the day and night. Members of the downtown live-in community need many of the same facilities as do those in the outlying neighborhoods, though in some cases they can use the larger facilities designed to serve the whole town. Since compactness is of the essence, some facilities, such as community gardens and playing fields, are not appropriate within the town center itself, though they might be provided adjacent to it.

Establishments requiring much space and relatively little contact with the public, such as automotive sales and service facilities, major industries, and the city equipment yard, should more logically be located toward the outer part of the town rather than at the town center.

Downtown Monrovia is among the many revitalized town centers in California.

Revitalization of town centers in existing urban areas and construction of town centers in areas with new urban growth are major goals of sustainable planning that can result in increased richness of people's existence. Fortunately, there is increasing activity in this area today. Both large and small communities throughout the United States are beginning to work on bringing back their downtowns.

Hayward, an older city adjacent to Oakland in the San Francisco Bay Area, provides an example of the rewards of such efforts. In 1992, Hayward's mayor, Michael Sweeney, was lamenting the decline of the place that was his own hometown. Families and middle-class residents in general were leaving the community, leading to an economic decline that was visually apparent. The city's streets were clogged by traffic, particularly at commute time, and the downtown area had deteriorated. The solution Sweeney conceived to address these problems has had time to be implemented and tested. It is working.

Sweeney's idea was to take advantage of the fact that there was a train stop for the San Francisco Bay Area Rapid Transit District (BART) not far from the center of town. The site was dominated by surface parking, and though it was adjacent to Hayward's Main Street, it was disconnected. No train commuter would think of walking downtown. Sweeney led the development of a plan to turn the area around the train stop into a civic plaza and mixed-use center, tying in an existing library and post office. The city has completed several elements of the plan, including a beautiful new city hall, a bus mall, and eighty-five town houses. Still to be built are more office space and housing at the site and a structured parking lot with retail establishments at street level. Private investors are building a supermarket in the area, along with a multiplex theater and additional housing. The developer of proposed upscale housing expressed confidence that downtown Hayward will be a great neighborhood. Both the expense of owning a car and the unpleasantness of traffic jams are now avoidable for those who live in this great new neighborhood, and the city of Hayward has regained its heart.

The new urbanism movement has spurred the inclusion of neighborhood and town centers in a number of new large-scale residential developments. For instance, at Haile Plantation near Gainesville, Florida, a developer is completing a new, one-third-mile-long Main Street as the town center of a 1,700-acre master-planned community. The developers waited until about 1,000 homes had been built so that they had the critical mass of people needed to support the undertaking. The results have been excellent. The attractive narrow, tree-shaded downtown street is lined by more than forty buildings, including shops, a corner grocery store, a dry cleaner, a post

The town center of Haile Plantation, a new master-planned community in Florida, has proven an economic success. (Photograph courtesy of Haile Plantation Corporation)

office, a dentist's office, and a stockbroker's office. The developer commented, "They came to us, so there must be a demand for our kind of Main Street."[11]

A few cities have demonstrated that automobile-oriented suburbs can be retrofitted with town centers. The village of Schaumburg, Illinois, provides an example. It has more than 74,000 residents, more than 75,000 jobs, and one of the world's largest enclosed shopping malls—but until recently it had no central place that residents could call their own. Schaumburg's village government decided to fix the situation. It assembled a twenty-nine-acre site (which included a failed retail center) and developed a town square master plan for the area with a new park ringed by buildings for retail, commercial, and civic uses, including a sixty-five-foot clock tower. In 1995, the city started selling off parcels to developers. Schaumburg's mayor, Al Larson, said, "We just wanted to create a plan reflecting our vision for the site and the community, then sell parcels to developers who would build our vision." At last report, the vision was coming to fruition.[12]

Many years ago, author Jane Jacobs wrote in *The Death and Life of Great American Cities*, "Without a strong and inclusive heart, a city tends to become a collection of interests isolated from one another. It falters at producing something greater socially, culturally, and economically than the sum of its separated parts."[13] After ignoring her advice for many years, the residents and leaders of many existing communities and the planners and developers of many new ones have decided she was right.

Circulation and Layout

Circulation systems within U.S. cities have traditionally been based on a grid pattern, with residential streets connected to larger arterial streets. Streets are designed for both cars and bicycles, which generally leaves the bicyclist at a disadvantage. Pedestrian walkways are along the sides of most of these streets. The pedestrian must cross the path of automobiles at every block and be subjected to noise and exhaust fumes. Because of the inability of the grid system to handle heavy flows of long-distance, high-speed through traffic, freeways are often added as a city expands.

In some instances, this works well, particularly where through traffic has been rerouted around a city to avoid interference with local traffic. It has not worked well, however, where expanding adjacent development has put more and more traffic onto neighborhood streets as people live farther and farther from the town center. Increased traffic flow on residential streets has tended to destroy older neighborhoods unless measures such as traffic calming and street closure have been implemented.

Where freeways have been built to accommodate commuter traffic, their presence has encouraged the continuation of sprawl by permitting developers to build in locations with access to freeways that are not yet congested during commuting hours. As building proceeds, the freeways gradually become more and more clogged for seemingly endless miles. This has led to commuters spending billions of frustrating hours in slow-moving lines of traffic, not to mention the resultant enormous drain on energy supplies.

Public transit systems should replace freeways as the major form of transportation in the future. (It is critical that we start planning now for the end of cheap gasoline rather than planning our transportation system around a resource that we know will not last.)

However, for public transit to work a community must be fairly compact. The closer people live to a train or bus stop, the more likely they are to use it. If the train or bus is a short and pleasant walk away, people will leave their cars at home and climb aboard. Transit service also must run frequently so that people do not have to stand around and wait.

To support frequent bus service, the general rule is that there must be a residential density of at least seven units per acre over an area of one-half

Downtown Portland, Oregon, has the densities and uses required to make public transit work.

square mile. For very frequent bus service, a community needs at least eight units per acre. To support light-rail service, a community should have forty-three units of housing per acre within one-eighth mile of a station and ten units per acre in the next one-eighth mile.[14] These figures are based on behavioral patterns during an era of very cheap gasoline and might be expected to change when gas prices inevitably rise.

To make bicycling and walking convenient means of transportation, a balance of residences, places of employment, entertainment facilities, and establishments offering goods and services must be provided in a compact scale and design that make these forms of transportation safe and pleasant. In order to create enjoyable pedestrian routes that are free of dangerous exhaust fumes, we believe it is sometimes preferable to keep automobile and pedestrian paths separate. At the same time, access for emergency vehicles must be available to all buildings, as must access for transport of items that cannot easily be carried.

The most obvious way to separate automobiles and people, and in fact the one used in Radburn, New Jersey, and in some other garden city plans, is to make all streets in the town feed outward to a peripheral ring road rather than inward. Bicycle and pedestrian paths, on the other hand, run inward from each neighborhood to the geographic center of town, where the transit stop and the commercial and civic facilities people visit most often are located. Vehicle access to the town center can be provided by a single service road bisecting the town and connecting at both ends to the ring road. With such a circulation system, one can reach any point in the town by automobile or travel between any two points, if necessary, by driving out to the ring road and around to the appropriate street entrance. This route is fairly indirect, however. Direct routes are reserved for bicyclists and pedestrians, for whom distance is more crucial. To keep these distances practical, the size of the town should be limited to four square miles or less. There should be higher-density development within and immediately adjacent to the town center. Around the town center can be neighborhoods of about 500 to 1,000 people, each surrounded by a greenbelt consisting of agricultural areas, parks, playing fields, and natural areas. It is interesting to note that the residents of Columbia, Maryland, a community designed along these lines, drive thirty fewer miles per month than do residents of neighboring communities.[15] Studies of European garden cities show similar results.

Laying out a community in this way creates an automobile-free living environment. The plan also lends itself easily to other design solutions, such as the creation of distinct neighborhoods adjacent to open spaces where food supplies can be grown and where, if conditions permit, treated wastewater can be used for subsurface irrigation. The plan makes it simple to incorporate natural drainage systems because there is open space adjacent to all buildings. The interconnection of open spaces allows for continuous waterways.

This basic pattern, a version of Ebenezer Howard's garden city, appears somewhat rigid in the accompanying conceptual drawing but can take on a limitless variety of forms based on terrain and other design constraints and concepts.

The Village Homes subdivision offers just one example of how automobile access can be provided for every home while maintaining a generally automobile-free neighborhood. (The Davisville project described in chapter 10 demonstrates how to accomplish this on a larger scale.) Because private yards have been created on the street side, we have been able to eliminate traditional fenced backyards and turn the property behind homes into a common open space—which then provides space for the bicycle paths and footpaths (as well as the channels that make up the natural drainage system).

Another important consideration in laying out the streets and paths of a neighborhood is that all structures should be able to take maximum advantage of the sun for space and water heating. Streets should be curved to avoid

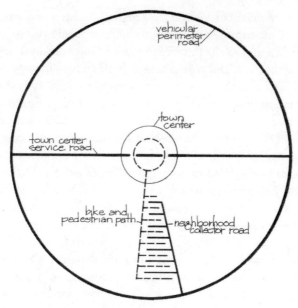

This conceptual circulation system shows direct pedestrian bike access in dashed lines and indirect auto access in solid lines.

An overview of Village Homes shows how solar orientation and curved streets can work together. (Photograph courtesy of Chad Ankele)

the somewhat undesirable visual effect of straight rows of houses all facing south. As in Village Homes, curved streets allow the houses to be staggered yet still maintain a southern orientation.

A couple of additional points seem important to the general layout of a neighborhood designed to reduce automobile traffic. Very small commercial centers should be located adjacent to or within each neighborhood so that daily needs can be met by walking. The variety and number of these should be based on the design of the local neighborhood as it grows and residents determine what their needs are.

In lieu of sidewalks on the street, 6-foot-wide paths can be used between groups of houses. This width seems to work well in Village Homes. The paths can lead into 8- and 10-foot-wide collector paths designed to carry more traffic.

In the more centralized parts of a town, heavily used arterial paths should probably be 12 to 24 feet wide. If automobile traffic gets to be heavy at intersections, stop signs or possibly a traffic circle may be required.

Street width can be drastically reduced in a development that encourages pedestrians and bicyclists because of the reduction in use of automobiles. Since the 1960s, street-width standards in the United States have become

Traffic circles slow automobiles, creating a safer environment for pedestrians.

ridiculously large, resulting in wasted land, to say nothing of the expense of development and maintenance.

The 20- and 26-foot-wide streets in Village Homes are city maintained. Our 20-foot-wide streets are more than adequate. The city mandated three-foot easements on either side, and obstructions and vegetation can be no more than six inches high in these areas. This allows for emergency access and walking room. Collector streets are also reduced in width. A minor arterial street adjacent to Village Homes is 38 feet wide. It has two 11-foot-wide automobile lanes and two 8-foot-wide emergency strips that also serve as bicycle lanes. At intersections, the street widens to accommodate an extra turning lane.

Nationally recognized street expert Dan Burden wrote a manual, published and distributed by the Local Government Commission, that provides guidance on street widths. Prepared after a nationwide review of neighborhood street design, the book defines three types of streets: those that provide neighborhood access, including trails, alleys, lanes, and streets; those that provide transitional access to neighborhood streets, such as avenues and main streets; and those that provide regional access, such as boulevards and parkways. The width of each is matched to desirable traffic speeds in the cor-

This fourteen-foot-wide street in Philadelphia functions well. (Photograph courtesy of Dan Burden)

responding area—with an emphasis on the safety and enjoyment of the pedestrian rather than facilitation of high-speed traffic. Burden's suggested street widths are as follows:

- Trail for nonmotorized access: 8 to 14 feet
- Alley providing access to the rear of a property: 10 to 12 feet
- Lane providing access to single-family homes: 16 to 18 feet
- Residential street: 26 feet
- Avenues connecting town centers and neighborhoods, with parking: 48 feet
- Main street with parking: 36 feet[16]

Although it is very difficult to get along without an automobile in today's world, which is designed for automobiles rather than for people, it would not be so in a world designed primarily for pedestrians, bicycles, and mass transit.

Appropriate Uses of Landscaping

Historically, our ancestors first exploited and then learned to manage the plants in their environment to meet important human needs. They used plants for food, fiber, and fuel and for protection from sun and wind, to hedge cattle in and enemies out, and to define social spaces. They also learned to manage plants to delight the senses with color and fragrance, the sound and movement of windblown foliage, and the order and complexity of natural forms. We believe that these pleasures go deeper than mere aesthetics; we believe they reflect the fact that human perceptions and responses are genetically tailored to the natural environment and to living things, and therefore such environments nurture people. Humans learned to manage their landscape environment to meet all these needs simultaneously in an integrated way.

The word *landscaping* has different connotations today. Both as generally practiced and as taught in most schools of landscape architecture, landscaping has little to do with protection from climate and nothing at all to do with production of food, fuel, or fiber. Its aesthetics often reflect fads. This kind of landscaping can be a wasteful practice.

To make landscaping an element of sustainable design, efforts must be made to rediscover the art of landscaping to satisfy diverse human needs simultaneously, making it an expression both of efficiency and of care for the ecosystem. In this section, we discuss in detail two aspects of this: landscaping for climate control and landscape productivity.

Landscaping for Climate Control

Plants are invaluable for controlling sun and wind and, in cold-winter climates, for controlling drifting snow. The most obvious example of wind control is a large-scale windbreak of tall trees that reduces wind speeds for long distances in its lee and for many times the height of the trees. But smaller plantings are also useful for more detailed control, either by moderating the wind's force or by controlling its direction. Relatively small plantings near a building can reduce wind speed next to the building by diverting wind around or over it. Foliage against the wall of a building—tall shrubs or a trellis with vines—can further reduce wind speed to create a virtual dead-air space next to the wall, which significantly reduces heat loss through the wall in cold weather. Shrubs can also provide wind protection for outdoor living spaces and entrances to buildings.

In hot climates, proper landscaping can improve ventilation of buildings by means of plantings planned for detailed control of wind direction. Landscape architect Robert F. White's studies at the Texas Engineering Experiment Station, published in 1945 and often reproduced, show in detail how various combinations of trees, shrubs, and hedges planted beside or upwind of a building can increase or reduce airflow through the building, change patterns of circulation within the building, or even reverse the direction of flow.[17] This knowledge can be particularly valuable in locations where wind directions are fairly regular. Around Davis, for example, because of the north–south orientation of the Sacramento Valley and its relationship to the Carquinez Strait air corridor, the summer breeze blows predictably from the north in the morning and from the south in the evening. In hilly areas, wind patterns may be more complex, but they are still fairly predictable in any one spot. Thus, landscaping for ventilation control calls for a familiarity with the patterns around each house that is available only to someone who lives there.

Where summers are warm, shading is an important goal of landscape plantings. Good shading can keep temperatures comfortable both indoors and outdoors. It can also save energy by reducing or eliminating the need for artificial air-conditioning. In the paragraphs that follow, we discuss shading in some detail because it can be particularly complicated around houses that use solar energy.

Everyone knows that it is more comfortable to be in the shade on a hot day because one's body is directly heated by solar radiation when in the sun. What is not so obvious is that lack of overall shading raises temperatures throughout the neighborhood, even in the shady places. Unshaded pavement—in streets, parking lots, patios, and walkways—is particularly troublesome in hot climates. Pavement is often dark colored and therefore absorbs more of the radiation that strikes it than do lighter surfaces. It does not cool itself by evaporation of water as vegetation does. Moreover, its mass stores heat during the day, so it remains hot well into the evening. A study conducted in Davis by the University of California showed that ambient temperatures are as much as ten degrees lower in neighborhoods where streets are well shaded than in those where street shading is poor.[18] Studies carried out in Sacramento by the Local Government Commission have confirmed this finding.

Streets, parking lots, and other large paved areas such as school playgrounds should not be designed without consideration of how they can be shaded. In Village Homes, we made streets easier to shade by eliminating parking lanes on either side and substituting intermittent angled parking bays with four parking spaces each. Thus, shade trees could be planted between bays or between a bay and a private driveway, separated only by the two travel lanes, with a total width of only twenty to twenty-six feet. This narrow street width allows us to completely shade the street with a tree canopy in summer.

Another design method—common in older neighborhoods and newer

Narrow, tree-shaded streets help keep Village Homes residents cool without the use of air conditioners.

Green edges on this street provide room for shade trees. (Photograph courtesy of Dan Burden)

ones designed according to new urbanist principles—places trees in a land-scaped buffer between the sidewalk and the street. This requires green edges of six feet or more on each side and street trees with foliage broad enough to create a double canopy, although the city of Seattle has had success with three-foot planting strips for certain tree species. Even a four-lane street can be completely shaded by putting a median strip in the center and planting it with trees.

Trees can also be used to make streets safer. Comparisons show that traffic on many tree-lined streets moves ten to fifteen miles per hour slower than does traffic on streets not lined with trees. Moreover, there is a direct correlation between traffic speed and seriousness of accidents.[19]

At the same time, however, trees must not substantially shade rooftop solar heat collectors or south-facing windows that function as solar heat collectors in winter. As discussed later in this chapter, deciduous trees can provide shade in summer, when solar space heating is not needed, because they lose their leaves in the fall and allow sunlight to reach the collectors or windows through the bare branches. But some deciduous trees do not lose their leaves early enough in some climates. Collectors used for domestic water heating work year-round, so they must never be shaded. Thus, shade plantings require careful planning. Landscape designers must be familiar with leaf-fall dates and growth patterns of various species in the local climate and must be able to use them creatively to provide shade or sunlight where and when it is needed.

In addition, advice by the neighborhood group as a whole concerning landscaping on private lots is necessary to make sure that plantings on one lot do not shade a neighbor's solar collectors. This can be accomplished with a provision for solar rights in the Declaration of Covenants, Conditions, and Restrictions (CC&Rs) of the subdivision or by local ordinance or state law. Village Homes has a section on solar rights in its CC&Rs:

> Whereas, that certain Declaration of Covenants, Conditions and Restrictions was recorded on October 31, 1975, as instrument No. 15574, in Book 1166, Page 385 of official records.
>
> Now therefore, the lot owners and the declarant Village Homes, do hereby modify said Declaration of Covenants, Conditions and Restrictions as follows:
>
> SOLAR RIGHTS
>
> All south-facing glass and solar space heating collectors in each house shall remain unshaded from December 21 to February 21 between the hours of 10 AM and 2 PM (solar time), except as provided herein.
>
> All roof-top solar hot water collectors on each house shall remain unshaded each day of the year between the hours of 10 AM and 2 PM (solar time), except as provided herein.
>
> Shading caused by the branches of deciduous trees shall be exempt from this restriction.
>
> Shading caused by original house construction, or fences built within six (6) months of occupancy shall be exempted from this restriction only upon special approval of the Village Homes Design Review Board.
>
> Homeowners may encroach upon their own solar rights.
>
> The Board of Directors of the Village Homeowners' Association shall have the authority to enforce this restriction.

It is particularly crucial to shade windows from direct sunlight during summer because any sunlight that falls on them enters the building and immediately turns into heat. Indoor curtains or blinds help little unless they are light in color to reflect solar radiation and fitted to the walls to prevent heat from sneaking into the room. Most of the light that strikes curtains or blinds turns into heat just as it would if allowed to cross the room and strike the opposite wall. Once the sun's energy passes through the glass, it is in, and it will raise the temperature of the room.

With thoughtful planning, deciduous shrubs and vines can shade windows as effectively as artificial shading devices such as awnings, and they can do it much more cheaply and attractively. Such vegetation is particularly valuable for shading south-facing windows used for solar heating because the foliage provides more shade in fall than it does in spring, when leaves are just beginning to form. Therefore, it can be arranged to shade the windows in fall, when the sun is lower in the sky but the weather is still warm, and admit sunlight in spring, when the sun is at the same angle but the weather is cool. A fixed awning or overhang used for the same purpose would give too much shade in spring or too little in fall.

Landscape Productivity: Food and Fuel

Landscaped spaces in our towns and suburbs today are almost entirely unproductive. This is a relatively recent development; a few centuries ago, it was quite common for each house to have its own garden, fruit trees, and vines. Small fields, forests, orchards, and vineyards surrounded towns so closely as to be part of the immediate landscape. The pattern still exists in many small old European towns.

This was a very efficient use of land. The same pieces of land provided both the space needed for growing food and fuel and the pleasant public and private outdoor territories needed for human activity, interaction, and comfort. Productive trees, bushes, and vines performed the same functions as do the unproductive ones now generally used in landscaping: providing shade, wind protection, and privacy; defining spaces; and creating a pleasing atmosphere by echoing the natural environment in which humans evolved.

Our present neglect of productive landscaping is wasteful in a number or ways. It not only wastes land but also wastes the energy and resources used in transporting and marketing agricultural products. It wastes fertilizer (which requires additional energy if chemically produced) and water where irrigation is required. It also wastes human labor. Unproductive landscaping requires about as much labor from the homeowner as does productive landscaping, but at the same time it requires others to work to produce the food elsewhere and to process and distribute it.

Suburbanites accustomed to purely decorative landscaping tend to assume that vegetable gardens are unsightly. A sprawling, neglected garden can be an eyesore, but in a relatively dense residential area where lots are small and garden space is at a premium, gardens are less likely to be neglected. With the garden right under the window and on public display, there is no reason to think that the homeowner will neglect its appearance, any more than he or she would neglect the appearance of a purely decorative yard.

As described in chapter 2, we reversed the typical neighborhood pattern in Village Homes by encouraging people to put their fenced private yards on the side of the house facing the street and requiring them to leave the yards on the other side open to a narrow common strip between the two rows of lots. The common strip is managed collectively by the homeowners on either side. People tend to do their gardening on the part of their lots facing this common strip or, by mutual agreement, on the common strip itself. Some groups of homeowners have developed very creative ways of integrating vegetable gardens with individual or communal patios or children's play areas. Because they are on the "public" side of the houses, owners tend to keep their gardens as well maintained as people in a standard subdivision keep their front yards. In fact, they experience similar social pressure from their neighbors to keep these publicly visible areas neat.

Nut trees, fruit trees, and fruiting shrubs and vines present no more neatness problems than do unproductive landscape plants. With their diverse sizes and growth habits, one or another of them can be used in almost any landscaping situation. Apple, filbert, fig, and apricot trees, with their spreading growth patterns and different sizes, are suitable for shading patios of various sizes. Trees with a more upright pattern—plum, cherry, and pear—are good for protection from the afternoon summer sun. In mild-winter climates, citrus trees, which do not lose their leaves, can provide a year-round windbreak or visual barrier. All of these trees are available in dwarf and semidwarf varieties that can be used in landscaping like medium-sized or large shrubs. Other species, such as blueberries and currants, grow naturally as shrubs. The smaller fruit and nut trees can be planted in rows and pruned flat to form a unified hedge or tall barrier, or they can be trained in the very flat and formal espalier style, hugging a fence or shading an east or west wall. The bramble fruits—raspberry, blackberry, and boysenberry—can be trained on supports to make a high or low fence. There are also plants considered primarily ornamental, such as crab apple and jujube, that bear edible fruit.

Grapevines are exceptionally versatile. In virtually any climate, some variety of grape can be grown and eaten fresh or made into raisins or juice. Grapevines can be trained on supports to make a low fence or on a vertical or overhead horizontal trellis to provide shade just where it is needed. They are particularly suitable for summer shading above the south-facing windows of a passive solar house. Kiwi vines (Chinese gooseberries) can be equally

Grapevines shade south-facing windows in Village Homes while providing tasty morsels for a snack.

useful in appropriate climates, and their sweet, egg-sized fruit are a special delicacy.

Public areas can also be landscaped with productive plants. In addition to the varieties already mentioned, the larger nut trees, such as walnut and pecan, can be used for large-scale shade. In Village Homes, we have allowed wild cherries, *Rosa rugosa,* and blackberries to grow wild along some of the natural drainage channels and in other areas. Tiny orchards and vineyards here and there in residential areas provide a bit of openness and relief from the continuous pattern of houses and lots.

It is important to realize that in many climates, the urban landscape is capable of producing food in economically significant quantities. In these days of large-scale mechanized agriculture, it is easy to write off as insignificant the yield of a peach tree here, two grapevines here, and a half dozen tomato plants there. But 100 peach trees scattered through a neighborhood of 1,000 persons are as productive as 100 trees in a one-acre orchard, and 1,000 such neighborhoods can produce as much as a 1,000-acre peach orchard. Moreover, those neighborhoods need not produce peaches alone; they may also have space for apples, pears, plums, apricots, and cherries; for nuts and berries and grapes; and for a wide variety of fresh vegetables in season.

A pear tree enhances a landscape while providing fruit for the residents of this house.

An important advantage of neighborhood agriculture is that it allows for a healthy ecological balance that cannot be maintained in large-scale, single-crop plantings. Because plantings of any one species are small and separate, they do not encourage pests of that species to build up a large population, and they make it harder for pests and diseases to spread. This makes it possible to avoid costly and environmentally destructive pesticides and to use natural controls instead. In Village Homes, orchards and vineyards are no larger than half an acre and are located next to landscaping that harbors enemies of their pests. For example, blackberries planted near vineyards harbor the *Anagrus* wasp, which preys on the grape leafhopper. Thickets are provided for birds that feed on insects, and small ponds allow insect-eating toads to complete their life cycles.

With the proper pollution control devices, firewood for heating and for generation of electricity may be an important part of our energy supply in coming years, and we could save additional energy by growing the trees near where the wood will be needed instead of hauling it for long distances. This makes it reasonable to consider forestland as a possible element in urban landscaping. Large and small woodlots could be placed in and around a town for firewood production, located so as to serve as windbreaks and harvested and replanted on a rotating basis. While the trees are growing, the woodlots could provide space for play, walking, jogging, picnics, and contemplation and serve as wildlife refuges. It would be possible to get away to the woods for half an hour at any time without driving great distances—or any distance at all.

In Davis, citizen activists have proposed that the city government create biomass forest areas around and within the city using eucalyptus, black locust, and other fast-growing species, interspersed with one- to twenty-acre organic truck farms. These areas would serve as buffer zones to protect the city from the drift of toxic agricultural chemical sprays.

Using Natural Drainage

The drainage of water from the land is an intricate process and an integral part of the ecosystem. It affects and is affected by the materials and contours of the ground and the living things in and on the ground, particularly plant life.

At the same time, however, natural drainage and the ecological communities related to it are a rich and satisfying part of humanity's subjective environment—aesthetically, sensually, and psychologically. It is subtly stimulating and comforting to experience the movement and sound of water in its

Water can add a great deal to the aesthetic appeal of a neighborhood.

great variety, flowing through almost-level fields, making its way along tiny creeks or swales, rushing down steeply inclined streams or over falls or rapids, or flowing smoothly and silently in deep, winding channels. The animal and plant life in these waterways and along their banks is endlessly fascinating. Every reader must have at least one memory of peaceful hours spent near naturally flowing water.

As a society, in building our towns and cities, we have done little or nothing to preserve natural drainage for either its aesthetic value or its ecological value. We have filled in existing waterways and have built so that runoff is collected immediately in street gutters and sent to underground drainage pipes or sewers. The natural streams we could not get rid of we have channeled into pipes, and then we have covered the pipes with dirt or asphalt. As the waterways have been destroyed, so have the plants and animals that lived along them. The accelerated storm runoff created by our propensity to channel rainwater rather than let it be absorbed into the ground creates enormous engineering problems, requiring huge holding ponds and, where sewers are used for storm drainage, oversized sewage plants.

After going to all the trouble and expense of eliminating natural waterways and wildlife habitats, we incur further expense in trying to build sterile substitutes back into our cities. We build fountains and fake pools and streams that use pumps to circulate the water. Some are bare concrete; others include plants and naturalistic landscaping, but because they are created by humans rather than by a balanced ecological process, they usually require constant maintenance. The very best one can say about these efforts is that they are a little bit better than having no running water at all.

Constructing a natural drainage system in a development like Village Homes, which has greenbelts running between the buildings, is simple. Lots are graded so that the streets and houses are higher than the creek running behind them. The water runs off the streets and houses and down into the creek. The system is engineered to hold more water than that expected in a 100-year storm, but walkways and vegetation along the creek and in the greenbelt will not suffer if they are covered by water on rare occasions. In a town center, the system is the same. Buildings are two-sided: one side faces the street, and the other is enhanced by the beauty of a nicely landscaped creek. Small dams can be constructed throughout the drainage system so that water can be held and the flow slowed during times of rapid rainfall. Mosquito fish are a necessary addition if water remains standing for more than three days, to ensure that mosquito larvae are eaten before they have a chance to hatch.

Maintenance of natural beauty and preservation of wildlife habitat are

Channeling of rivers destroys both beauty and habitat. (Photograph courtesy of Local Government Commission)

A more natural approach to water management seems far superior. (Photograph courtesy of Local Government Commission)

only two of the reasons for taking advantage of natural drainage systems. Doing so can also reduce costs, conserve water, reduce flooding problems, and actually increase property values.

Storm drains are expensive to build, operate, and maintain. Great savings can be realized by relying instead on human-made surface drainage swales and any natural waterways existing on the site. Because the water does not drop below ground level, no pumping station or energy is required to pump it back up. Blockages in a surface drainage system merely raise the water level instead of stopping the flow and are easily spotted and removed, whereas in a subsurface system they can put a storm sewer completely out of action and be difficult to find and clear.

Natural drainage also allows the ground to absorb and retain water, which is particularly beneficial in areas that have light annual rainfall. In California's Sacramento Valley, for example, the ground can absorb an entire winter's rainfall without becoming saturated to a depth from which the roots of grass, shrubs, and trees can recover the water. Therefore, any rainwater that can be made to soak into the soil instead of running off means an equivalent reduction in watering requirements during spring and fall. Native plants can often survive with no additional water at all. In wetter regions, water absorbed into the ground surface or into streambeds may eventually find its way into underground aquifers that supply water to wells. This is important because in many areas, the groundwater level is becoming alarmingly low as a result of increased pumping from wells for irrigation and domestic uses.

Modern drainage systems, on the other hand, tend to maximize runoff and carry the water to rivers or large streams or to evaporation ponds. Only in a few areas are recharge ponds used to get water into the ground and replenish the water table, and these do nothing to directly satisfy watering needs in the neighborhoods where the rain originally fell.

In areas with greater rainfall, natural drainage is valuable in evening out downstream flow rates. The many small waterways that contain water only during rains and for a few days afterward keep the water moving slowly and allow it to soak into the banks, where it is held and gradually released. Thus, rainfall reaches the larger streams gradually, over a period of many days. In neighborhoods where runoff is carried in street gutters and underground pipes, these natural delaying processes do not occur and rainfall reaches streams and rivers in a matter of hours. Storms produce sudden, heavy surges that can destroy small streams and create flooding problems in larger ones, requiring major artificial controls such as holding ponds and straightened channels. In towns where storm drainage enters the sewage system, these surges require sewage plants with absurdly large peak capacities, and even then, unusually heavy storms may force the dumping of untreated sewage into streams, rivers, or bays.

One thing engineers tend to overlook is that a view of a creek or pond increases the value of a home or neighborhood. In Davis, water from our part of town was pumped into an evaporation pond—just a square pond with sides too steep to support any wildlife. When Michael was mayor, he suggested turning the pond into a wildlife refuge by creating natural-looking contours and planting the area with native grasses and trees. Now the ditch seems to have turned into a parking place for many birds on the Western Flyway, and we constantly enjoy the sight and sound of ducks and geese overhead. The pond is a great place to go for a walk, and homes that overlook the area command premium prices. Other neighborhoods have gotten the message, and several similar drainage–wildlife refuge projects now exist throughout Davis.

When we were in our mid-twenties and living in San Anselmo, California, we decided to build a house for ourselves on a lot that had a small creek running across the back. We bought the lot, and when we were getting the building permit, an engineer from the Department of Public Works apolo-

A combination drainage pond and wildlife refuge in Davis, California, has proven to be a major asset to the community. (Photograph courtesy of Local Government Commission)

gized for the fact that the creek had not yet been replaced with an underground concrete pipe. When Michael told him that he preferred that the creek be left as it was, the engineer said that the city had a right-of-way across the property and would eliminate the stream sooner or later. During the time we lived in that house, we enormously enjoyed hearing the sound of the water and watching the deer that came to drink, the small trout in the pools in summer, and the steelhead spawning in winter. Fortunately, we sold the house before that wonderful natural amenity was covered over. Its loss definitely would have decreased the sales value of our home.

Village Homes and Davis are by no means the only place in the United States where natural drainage is being used successfully. Other communities are discovering the assets of natural drainage systems and uncovering previously buried or hidden creeks and streams. San Antonio, Texas, has for some time been taking full advantage of the stream running through the city by featuring it as a focal point of the community. Officials in San Luis Obispo, California, have enhanced their town center by doing the same. One can now dine on decks that overlook natural areas along the stream and enjoy walks on paths that line the area. Former Portland, Oregon, city council member Earl Blumenhauer, now a member of the United States Congress, has shared with us his public works efforts in Portland to return creeks to the light of day.

A natural creek and drainage area runs through a park in Ashland, Oregon, enhancing the park's aesthetic value.

In conclusion, we believe that the garden city as proposed by Ebenezer Howard more than a hundred years ago provides an excellent framework for a more sustainable urban form. With the addition of everything learned in the twentieth century about designing with nature for people, it provides us with a fine blueprint for a more sustainable and successful twenty-first century.

Chapter 9

The Process of Creating Sustainable Communities

Designing a new garden city or garden village neighborhood or redesigning an existing urban area requires the integration of many different requirements into a land use plan. The critical roles of aesthetics and citizen participation must also be considered. And most important, the plan must be implemented.

Earlier in the book, we examined the importance of location of the site: its climate, its proximity to other settlements and to natural resources, the availability of water, and the potential for dispersion of air pollution. We discussed analysis and mapping of the site's existing drainage patterns and natural aesthetic features and examination of its soil types, solar orientation, endangered habitat, and so on, to determine which locations are best suited to various uses: agriculture, forestry, sewage recycling, buildings, roads and paths, and parks. We discussed how these factors should determine the overall size and density of settlement the site can support.

We also looked at conceptual notions of what a settlement should ideally be like and how it should ideally be laid out—appropriate size for efficient government and a good social atmosphere, appropriate patterns of circulation, proper relationship between public and private spaces and between living and working spaces, and so on. We described a variety of technologies from which to choose—different ways of handling sewage, different ways of producing energy, and different materials and methods for constructing buildings.

At this point, however, theory and analysis can go no further. Successful integration of all these factors into a harmonious, elegant site plan depends on a designer or design team's creative ability and intuitive perception of comprehensive solutions. In the end, the design of a sustainable human environment will require sensitive artists who have a grasp of all aspects of the problem and all elements of the required solution. Designers must also draw on their own sense of line, space, proportion, pattern, and symbolism. Their ability to do so will make the difference between a profoundly beautiful and satisfying setting and one that is aesthetically and subjectively mediocre.

The Role of Aesthetics

Many years ago, when visiting a house designed by Frank Lloyd Wright, Michael became keenly aware of a pleasant feeling and realized that architecture should be judged by the way people feel when they are using the space. This criterion takes in both the functional and the aesthetic aspects of architecture. The functional aspects are fairly straightforward; people will feel less comfortable if the light glares in their eyes, if the temperature is too warm or cold for the amount of physical activity going on, if furniture is too high or too low, if there is too much or too little privacy, or if things are arranged to require unnecessary movement or to make circulation awkward. But there are more subtle and subjective factors that affect people's comfort and mood within urban spaces and determine the ambience of those spaces. Some of the factors may be purely symbolic, such as an orderly design that symbolizes an orderly and dependable world; a broad porch and a pleasant, accessible walkway that symbolize welcome; house plants that symbolize life, growth, and nurturing; or some shape that has special meaning within a culture. Other design elements may contribute to a pleasant ambience by echoing the natural forms among which humans evolved. Others may have meanings or meet subtle human needs of which even the designer is only intuitively aware.

Our visits to successful communities in Europe and the United States have underscored for us the importance of aesthetic considerations not only in home design but also in neighborhood and community design. Some public spaces are delightful, exciting, wonderful places to be—the plazas of Paris, the streets of Barcelona, the village greens in England, the paseos in Santa Barbara, the squares in Boston—whereas the look-alike strip developments and big-box retail centers found everywhere across the United States are barely tolerable places to spend time.

We believe it is not enough for the designer to be intellectually knowledgeable about human needs and ways of meeting them or even to be skilled at integrating a variety of needs into a single harmonious, elegant solution. To masterfully design nurturing spaces, one must also be intuitively sensitive to the ambience of spaces: the shades of mood and feeling that spaces evoke

A great public marketplace in Boston.

and the meanings they suggest. The designer must be able to arrange spaces to evoke the desired feeling, meaning, and mood, just as the poet must be able to arrange words to evoke the desired feeling and understanding in a reader's mind. The designer's task differs from the poet's only in that the elements he or she works with, unlike words on paper, must also perform concrete physical and social functions. The solutions must integrate ambience and function.

So much of the human-made environment is created without thought for visual consequences. We wonder sometimes whether this is not a sociological time bomb. People had been tampering with the physical environment for many years before the long-range detrimental effects of those manipulations, such as global warming, became obvious. The same may be true for changes in the subjective environment. It is possible that people have not yet begun to understand the negative effects of visual environments that have an oppressive ambience. Many of the problems that plague society today, such as "road rage," may stem in part from such subjective factors.

There are countless design theories, philosophies, and styles that address the subjective aspect of architectural design. We will not go into them here except to mention two that we believe stand out. One is the traditional Japanese style, which emphasizes simplicity, subtlety, use of natural materials and naturalistic landscaping, and the relationship between the building

Strip development fails to provide community spaces. (Photograph courtesy of Local Government Commission)

and the garden. The second is the view expressed by John Ruskin in *The Poetry of Architecture*.[1] Ruskin praises the architecture of simple, unpretentious buildings of the eighteenth and nineteenth centuries. European cottages and villas of this era, he says, demonstrate that beauty is born in the simplicity of a design solution and matures with the aging of a building as the building serves its function well and shows signs of use.

We believe that there is also a great deal to be said for an order and consistency in neighborhood and community design that extends to a consistency in the appearance of homes. We are not talking about the monotonous fundamental uniformity of tract homes, poorly masked by random variations in color and style of facade, but rather the opposite: a fundamental variation and individuality in design overlain with a harmonious thematic consistency. This can be seen and felt in the ambience of old European towns and more primitive villages, where consistency developed naturally through emulation and tradition, a limited variety of available materials, and an absence of rapid change in building technology.

Consistency in building style has a lot of desirable symbolism. It provides our connection to the history of the place. It suggests that good solutions do not change, that they are not arbitrary, and that appropriate materials are not arbitrary. On a deeper level, it symbolizes the possibility that unique indi-

Many European towns have a pleasant thematic consistency in their architecture.

viduals can join together into harmonious communities and societies without losing their basic individuality. It symbolizes a cooperative spirit and respect and consideration for one's neighbors and the community as a whole.

Consistency in building style also echoes the world of nature. Consider peach trees: no two are alike, but there is a fundamental consistency in shape, color, and growth pattern that makes it easy to distinguish any peach tree from a palm tree or a rosebush or even from members of more closely related species, such as apple and plum trees. Landforms and types of rock also exhibit this patterned variation. If it is true that human perception is by evolution adapted to natural forms, then it is probably also adapted to allow us to detect the subtle patterns of these forms. Since we generally find pleasure in the exercise of our capacities, it is likely that we would experience such patterned variation as pleasurable, whether we find it in peach trees or in houses.

The greatest potential for achieving unified neighborhood design may lie not in stricter authoritative control but in people becoming aware that there are optimum materials and design techniques for particular locations and that there are aesthetic advantages and delights to a neighborhood created by a good designer using the materials most appropriate for that location.

Although an overall continuity of design is important, it is also very important for residents to be involved in creation of the overall design and, indeed, in any decision affecting the community. This helps the designer meet the residents' needs, but equally important, it gives residents a sense of their ability to help shape their community and a feeling that the community is truly theirs.

Citizen Participation

Involving citizens in the design process does complicate the designer's job. This may be why continuity in large-scale designs often seems to be achieved at the expense of user participation. On the other hand, user participation without adequate designer coordination has produced chaotic, unpleasant environments. One must steer a middle course here.

The procedures we used in the design of Village Homes provide a useful example of such a middle course. Our general strategy was to begin with an overall plan and a set of planning concepts and leave the details to be worked out as development progressed, with as much input from users as possible at each stage.

As mentioned in chapter 2, many of the ideas we implemented in Village Homes originated among a small number of people brought together to plan a community as a group. By the time the group dissolved, its meetings and discussions had helped us develop a general concept of what a neighborhood should be.

Two years later, when the way opened for us to develop a sixty-acre parcel of land on the edge of Davis, we developed this concept into a master plan for the site. We then presented the plan to friends, acquaintances, and prospective home buyers and investors to get their reactions. Their feedback was used to refine the plan.

The plan we presented to the city showed streets, lots, open spaces, and sites for recreational and commercial facilities but left the details of buildings and landscaping to be determined as the project proceeded with input from homeowners. New homeowners participated in the design of greenbelts and common areas adjacent to their homes. As the neighborhood grew, members also helped decide which community facilities should be built and finalized their design.

Similar procedures can be used in designing new towns and redesigning existing urban spaces into viable communities. A designer or design team familiar with general social, environmental, and aesthetic considerations can talk with people representative of those for whom he or she is planning to get a sense of their particular needs and desires. Then, on the basis of available technologies and the characteristics of the site and drawing on his or her knowledge of design concepts, the designer can develop a master plan and a set of architectural and landscaping guidelines, leaving detailed design to be determined during development with further input from residents. Before development begins, however, the master plan and guidelines can be refined through feedback gained in further talks with representative users.

Since the completion of Village Homes, there has been an increasing awareness of the importance of involving residents in the planning and design process. Research shows that direct participation in, for instance, the simple act of planting a tree is associated with greater satisfaction with one's neighborhood than when trees are planted by the city, the developer, or volunteer groups without involvement of the residents.[2]

In the past, it has been difficult or impossible to get the average citizen interested or involved in the urban planning process because of the difficulty of conceptualizing the end result by means of two-dimensional sketches or legal zoning and planning jargon. Because of this, few people show up for public hearings. Efforts to address this challenge have led to the recent development of some excellent citizen participation tools.

One of these tools, now used extensively by the Local Government Commission, is the Community Image Survey, based on the Visual Preference Survey created by architect Anton Nelessen. It consists simply of asking people to rate slides using a scale of plus 1 to 10 for a positive reaction and a scale of minus 1 to 10 for a negative reaction. We have found this to be extremely valuable in helping people focus on the environment around them in order to understand what they like and dislike, what their choices are, and how design can be used to make their communities better.[3] The Community Image Survey has been used in such cities as Reno, Nevada; Portland, Oregon; and Truckee, California to help produce general plans and design guidelines that are understood and supported by their residents.

Another, more expensive tool is computer simulation. Using computer technology, people can see, for example, what their street would look like if it were narrowed, if trees were added, or if height restrictions were imposed. This technique was used by the city of Orlando, Florida, to involve residents in the creation of a master plan to revitalize three declining neighborhoods in the Parramore Heritage District, the home of most of the city's African American community. Workshops were held for each neighborhood, bringing in merchants, homeowners, tenants, property owners, and elected officials. The ultimate goal of each workshop was to answer the question "Parramore, what do you want to be?" Using computer simulation, citizens could see the results of proposed design and policy changes. This piqued people's

*The Community Image Survey helps people articulate what they do and do not like.
(Photographs courtesy of Local Government Commission)*

interest in participating, assisted them in making more informed decisions, and helped them reach consensus.[4]

A very low-cost citizen participation technique was devised by a planner in the city of Olympia, Washington, to solve a problem of much larger scale—where to locate the 4,200 new households expected in the city by the year 2015. Participants were given photographs of well-designed housing types that fit into the local architectural vernacular so that they could see what housing might look like at various densities, from 2.5 units per acre to 35 units per acre. After this, groups of participants were given a simple map of the area—like a game board—and colored squares denoting different densities. As the "game players" attempted to fit the projected growth into the acreage provided, the trade-off between various housing densities and parks and open space became obvious.[5] Game players might also address issues such as neighborhood parks versus large parks and proximity of housing to services or public transit.

To bring it all together, the process of designing sustainable communities

Computer simulation allows people to visualize planning ideas, such as changes in the design of a street. (Photographs courtesy of Sierra Business Council)

requires the use of geographic information systems (GIS) technology to prepare an integrated design solution; it requires strong artistic talent on the
part of the urban planner, landscape architect, or architect to make the end
result satisfying to the senses; and it requires involvement of citizens in the
process to ensure an appropriate design and the development of community
ownership and pride. If these steps are followed, society will enjoy the multiple benefits of more sustainable and emotionally satisfying communities.

Implementation by Local Government

The process of planning sustainable garden cities will differ from current
planning procedures in two main ways. First, it will direct attention in planning to a number of social, environmental, and economic factors that have
been virtually ignored in current planning. Second, it will develop comprehensive plans for areas at a much earlier stage of development; in fact, planning will have to be done prior to any approvals. This will lead to better
planning because planning issues are more effectively addressed when a plan
is developed as a whole than when it is pieced together from unrelated proposals submitted over a number of years by different developers. With a
comprehensive plan already laid out, governmental evaluation and approval
of developers' proposals will be simpler and quicker, saving money and time
for both government and developer. The developer will also benefit from
knowing more clearly in advance what sort of proposal the government will
find acceptable. The reduction of red tape and time delays and the assurance
of good environmental decisions could ease some tensions and open the
door to a more unified effort between the traditionally opposing forces of the
development industry and environmentalists.

The most effective way to approach this kind of planning is to coordinate it with the development of regional plans. This can be done if jurisdictions within a region agree to update their general plans at the same time.
Whether this occurs or, as is usually the case, a city or county updates its general plan independently, the following steps should be taken:

1. Define the planning boundary. (It might be a city, a county, or a region
   incorporating a number of jurisdictions.)

2. Determine what land should be set aside as unbuildable open space.

3. Designate areas to be developed as garden cities and garden villages on
   the basis of their ability to produce an efficient public transit system,
   both within the living area and in relation to the larger regional transportation system. (The San Diego Association of Governments, Port-

land Metro, the city of Portland, and others are currently designating areas around transit stations for higher-density development.)

4. Produce specific plans for each garden city or garden village prior to any development within its bounds.

Development should not be approved by any jurisdiction until a specific or precise plan is complete, to ensure that the result will be a complete community or part of an effort to establish a complete community rather than the usual piecemeal urban sprawl. An example of this process can be found in the city of Oakdale, California, which incorporated the Ahwahnee Principles in its general plan. At the same time, the city established a policy that new growth could take place only in specified areas and that prior to development approval, the developer must prepare a specific plan consistent with those principles.

One obstacle to this kind of planning is that someone has to lay out money for preparation of the specific or precise plan a number of years before there is any development income to cover it. In some cases, developers or landowners will organize to finance a specific plan if they believe that they will not be allowed to develop without one. In many cases, however, city or county governments will have to provide the initiative. Some cities already provide funds for specific plans and are reimbursed later by development fees.

Currently, funds authorized by the federal Transportation Equity Act for the 21st Century (TEA-21) can be used for preparing a plan for mixed-use development around a transit stop. A few metropolitan planning organizations in California and Oregon also support such activities.

Although peculiarities of site and situation will make every garden city in some sense unique, there are considerations that apply to all of them.

For economic reasons, it is important to develop public services for a new garden city gradually, as it develops. With a comprehensive plan for the fully developed garden city in hand, it may be tempting for a government to require construction of the full-scale public facilities all at once. However, the interest on the capital required to do so is staggering and would significantly increase the price of homes. Any delays in development would make these interest costs even higher. Although development can in some cases pay for all the infrastructure necessary to support it, the infrastructure should be designed to avoid unnecessary costs and to be built in phases to avoid excessive expense.

Development should proceed cautiously and frugally. For example, when the new garden city sets up its fire and police forces, these can be housed temporarily in an inexpensive structure that will eventually become an equipment storage building for the public works department. The city government can initially share this building and later work out of a building that will ultimately be rented to private businesses for office space, either in the town center or in one of the neighborhood centers. A permanent police station, fire station, and city hall need not be built until the area is more than half developed and able to generate adequate revenue for its construction and maintenance. Similarly, the garden city's first school for all grades up to or including junior high can be a building that will eventually house only a few grades or serve only one or two neighborhoods.

The town's public infrastructure must reflect a real effort toward simplicity, frugality, and functionality. Some of the features we advocate for noneconomic reasons, such as narrow streets and surface storm drainage, will coincidentally save money, but planners must try to economize in all other areas as well. Designing more economically will require a conscious effort because public officials, engineers, architects, and planners, as well as citizens, will have developed their standards during a period of affluence. Reasonably priced housing cannot be built without such efficiencies.

Sustainable development is less costly than the standard development patterns of today. Patrick Condon, an associate professor in the Landscape Architecture Program at the University of British Columbia, working with the Fraser Valley Real Estate Board, the city of Surrey, British Columbia, and the Greater Vancouver Regional District, has studied the costs and benefits of "green infrastructure." The concept includes narrow streets, gravel lanes, and surface storm drainage systems linked to a preserved and enhanced natural drainage system. They found their proposed green infrastructure standards to be considerably more economical for the developer. For example, a traditional ten-and-one-half-acre project expanded to fourteen acres to produce a more sustainable development alternative would cost $90,000 less for the land, construction, and infrastructure.[6] The 1998 book *Green Development: Integrating Ecology and Real Estate,* written by the staff of the Rocky Mountain Institute, reports similar savings realized by those who have incorporated such measures in their development projects.[7]

The Local Government Commission has examined the fiscal effects of narrowing streets, providing natural drainage, and increasing the energy efficiency of housing through solar orientation and various conservation measures. A consultant developed a computer program for the commission that allows a city to input the amount and type of housing, desired street width, and other variables. Information about climate and utility prices is embedded in the program. Thus, the commission is now able to demonstrate the cost savings of these more sustainable design measures to the city, the developer, and the residents. In many cases, the savings are considerable.

A county in which a new garden city is to be located may want some sort of guarantee that the garden city will incorporate within a reasonable time or when it reaches a certain size. Ordinarily, a developing area cannot be incorporated unless the residents vote to incorporate, and when they are reluctant to do so, the county is saddled with the cost and responsibility of providing services and utilities on a scale beyond what it is equipped to handle. The most direct solution is for the county simply to require incorporation before it permits development to begin. It is also possible, however, to include a provision in the development's Declaration of Covenants, Conditions, and Restrictions (CC&Rs) that the garden city will be incorporated at some specified time. This way, each new resident will give consent to incorporation as part of the lot purchase transaction—it will be written into the deed, so no vote will be necessary at the time of incorporation.

It is usual for cities or counties to require subdivision developers, as part of the subdivision agreement, to donate to the public certain parcels of land within their subdivisions and certain improvements to those parcels—streets, sewer and water lines, land for parks, and the like—and to contribute through a development fee to city facilities outside the subdivision, such as central sewage plants. Although it is important that the local government not make development needlessly difficult by requiring too much too soon, it is also important that these contributions from the developer not be allowed to lag behind the general pace of development. This is necessary to avoid the danger of inflation or a developer's bankruptcy leaving the project without necessary public amenities such as schools and retail and office space. Therefore, there must be a careful plan of development for the entire garden city project stating just what is required from the developer at each stage. This agreement between the developer and the county also protects the developer from capricious changes in requirements, allowing him or her to plan ahead with confidence.

Equal attention must be given to development of a new garden city's economic base. Because ecological planning should minimize commuting, garden cities cannot rely on exporting labor as do today's bedroom communities. Therefore, they will require local businesses and industries that either produce goods for "export" or provide services—accounting, research, or computer services, for example—to outside businesses in addition to providing goods and services for community residents. Garden cities have a great drawing card for business: they offer a pleasant place for employees to live—a lively community with a beautiful setting, potentially clean air, little crime, and housing at competitive prices.

What is to prevent a garden city, once developed, from growing beyond its intended size? This is a particularly important question in a comprehensively planned community because additional growth would tend to undermine the benefits of the original good planning. For example, it could occupy land intended for food or biomass production or for recreation. Development outside the distance convenient for bicycling would tend to generate amounts of automobile traffic that would cause congestion in streets and parking areas designed only for light use. Therefore, local governments undertaking garden city–type planning must take steps to keep the communities from growing beyond the optimum size. In a new town planned from the very beginning to grow only to a certain size, no one could claim to have been taken by surprise. In addition, voters in a new town would tend to be aware of the town's development plan and the reasons behind it, and the disadvantages of further growth would be clearer to them than they would be to voters in a conventional town.

Still, in many cases it would be wise to set up further barriers to growth beyond the intended size. One method would be to tie up development options on land outside the planned borders of the town. For example, as of spring 1999, Boulder, Colorado, had purchased 28,907 acres surrounding the city. In a new town, this method should be easier because the options could be acquired before development raises their value. This could be done either by a special service district or by the developers themselves. Once all the necessary options are acquired, they could be placed in trust so that the land cannot be developed. Another way to preserve the planned size of a garden city, whether as a new city or as a district of an existing city, is to designate undeveloped land around the community as permanent open space in the general plan. The land value then would not escalate beyond the value of its current use, and this would increase the possibility that it would be affordable enough to ultimately be purchased by a land trust.

Overcoming Barriers to a Better Process

In any discussion of improving urban design, the question inevitably arises of why rational design processes are not in use already, why coherent plans are seldom made and are almost never followed, and what it would take to change that. Once we ask these questions, our attention turns to politics, government, law, finance, education, and culture and we find ourselves discussing procedures in a broader—very much broader—sense.

In general, the earliest human settlements evolved naturally from small groups of individuals who shared the same basic assumptions and goals. Because they had limited technology and resources, their choices were few. Moreover, technological change took place much more slowly, so the parameters of the design problem remained relatively constant, and this allowed a tradition of good design and successful solutions to develop. It was a process of trial and improvement, carried out in a much more informal and leisurely manner. The results were strikingly functional and aesthetic.

The process was somewhat more complicated in the planning of the earliest cities, but it was unified by the central power of rulers who could commission architects and planners to meld the needs of the various groups into a coherent design and execute it. Planning in Europe and the United States became more difficult as power was decentralized, interest groups became more divergent in their goals, and technological change occurred at a faster rate.

In the twentieth century, as discussed in previous chapters, many planners, architects, and social critics proposed the use of a more comprehensive design process. New towns built in the United States earlier in the century, such as Columbia, Maryland, and Reston, Virginia, created environments that are well organized as far as they have gone. The best plans put forward, including the English garden city concepts of Ebenezer Howard, were never executed to their full extent because they did not receive enough backing.

Although the 1990s brought some hopeful signs of progress in addressing ecology and community in a more comprehensive way, efforts toward sustainable community design are still far too rare. The few innovative developers who do want to produce more sustainable places for people to live face an uphill battle in getting new ideas implemented.

We believe that the basic problem is fragmentation of power and authority over the planning process. There is no unified planning authority demanding designs that integrate a variety of needs and goals. The power over planning is divided among many individuals, officials, and institutions, each concerned only with some small part of the total picture—bankers concerned only with profit and financial security, public engineers concerned only with efficient flow of sewage and traffic, and fire departments concerned only with reaching a fire quickly.

None of these problems is unimportant, but the official concerned with only one of them usually prefers to solve it in the easiest and most direct way. He or she has no responsibility for the overall plan and therefore no incentive to be creative or flexible in solving his or her own problem. The firefighter will want wide streets instead of considering smaller, more maneuverable fire engines; the banker will want to stick with plans that have been financially successful in the past. Any designer who wishes to see a comprehensive design adopted and executed today is likely to be forced into the role of educator, conducting special presentations or seminars for those in positions of authority to help them see beyond their individual areas of concern. At first, these efforts are likely to be met with some impatience or annoyance: "Why are you telling me all this? All I need to see is the sewer plan." Eventually, they may be rewarded with interest or even support, but a lot of patience and tenacity will be required, as well as the working capital needed to keep the project going in spite of constant delays.

We think that the real hope for improving urban design lies in planning entities developing more comprehensive design solutions that rely on both environmental information and citizen input. These entities should then be able to carry out their plans in the face of a certain amount of opposition from traditional outside authorities. At the same time, planning entities must gain authority over large enough regions to allow them to develop integrated, coherent regional plans. What is "large enough" depends on the sort of planning involved. For example, development of a coherent watershed plan for the Tennessee Valley required a planning entity covering portions of several states.

A regional planning approach therefore requires a hierarchy of planning entities. Regional planning agencies should locate growth sites both for new urban development and for redevelopment within existing cities. They should integrate all the pertinent information into one map using GIS. They should coordinate the planning for energy, water, agriculture, natural habitat preservation, recreation, and transportation within the region. Once the regional planning entity identifies a proper location, local planning agencies should handle the actual design of new towns (preferably planned as garden cities) or redevelopment areas under their jurisdiction. Within each of these local areas, there should be a community planning commission with jurisdiction over its own planning.

This hierarchy is intended to locate more of the decision making as close as possible to the place being affected, to allow for public input before major decisions are made, and to provide future users with more access to those who make the final decisions. This seems to be the most democratic way to approach planning. The planning process offers the greatest potential if the overall layout is designed in advance, including basic systems such as circulation, energy management, waste management, and major social services. As the settlement is developed, the more detailed design of individual buildings and neighborhoods is carried out by smaller planning groups that include residents and potential residents. Approached in this way, design can be an incredibly rich and satisfying process for everybody involved and can restore residents' feeling that their neighborhoods are truly their own. Such an approach can also permit enough diversity and experimentation in neighborhood design to demonstrate what works and what does not.

Comprehensive planning will be politically feasible only where the general public understands the goals and assumptions of good planning and where individuals are ready to speak out and take action to see that such planning is implemented. Therefore, the role of education, both formal and informal, cannot be overlooked. The relationship between people and the environment should be stressed in school in the earliest grades, and such education should be continued throughout a child's formal schooling. Films, books, and class curricula need to be expanded to include more in this area. Education of the general public must also take place. Again, films, books, courses, and seminars should be developed to broaden the public's knowledge.

The city of Davis became nationally recognized in the 1970s for its environmentally sound planning policies. It is no coincidence that the University of California, Davis, is the site of one of the country's first graduate programs in ecology. The citizens' group that was responsible for many of the city's innovations in energy planning was made up primarily of ecology graduate students. They so inspired and impressed the rest of the town with the urgency of responding to the energy and environmental crisis that constructive change became a possibility. Participating firsthand in the Davis experience taught us the value of a citizenry with a well-rounded education.

More recently, the city of Portland has become a model for better planning, admired by many across the country. This area of Oregon takes a regional approach to transportation, integrates transportation and land use planning, and has successfully limited urban sprawl and preserved farmland. The city has also taken the lead in downtown and neighborhood revitalization. This community places a high degree of emphasis on citizen education and citizen participation. Anyone who turns on a television set in Portland is likely to find a program in progress educating Portland's citizens about regional planning efforts. These examples demonstrate that communities that have educated citizens with a broader, more interdisciplinary outlook can make a transition from an unsustainable living environment to one that is ecologically sound.

Chapter 10

The Garden City: Case Studies of Sustainable Development in Practice

In this chapter, we give examples of how the garden city concept, updated to take into account ecological considerations and aspects of the new urbanism, can be adapted to most urban planning situations. We examine a garden city proposed for development adjacent to Davis, California, and two additional projects inspired by Village Homes—Prairie Crossing near Chicago and Civano in Tucson, Arizona. We also describe Haymount in Caroline County, Virginia, and Coffee Creek Center in Chesterton, Indiana. Finally, we discuss how the garden city concept is and could further be applied in the redevelopment of existing urban areas. In every case, the basic objective is to avoid piecemeal planning or planning by default and to plan at a large enough scale to produce a complete community.

Designation of garden cities is a formidable planning task in itself, particularly where they include or are adjacent to existing development. Garden cities cannot be laid out arbitrarily because part of the goal is to make new development complement existing development and to take advantage of whatever potential the existing development has for incorporation into a community and a comprehensive regional plan. Planners must try to make sense out of existing development and maximize its potential through careful designation of suitable size and boundaries for the ensured success of the garden city or garden village.

New Garden Cities

The process of getting governmental approvals and financing for a new garden city incorporating principles of sustainability is extremely difficult. We have identified three such efforts that appear to have surmounted the barriers. The fourth, Davisville, still must overcome some political obstacles.

193

Case Study—Haymount

The Haymount development appears to be one of the best examples of the sustainable garden city concept under construction to date. The developer, John Clark, and the planners, Andres Duany and Elizabeth Plater-Zyberk, began in 1988 by performing a site analysis for a 1,650-acre piece of property in Caroline County, Virginia, to determine where best to concentrate growth and which areas to preserve in farming and open space. Haymount is designed as a complete community with a population of 9,500. The plan provides for retail establishments and services to meet residents' daily needs, jobs in environmentally sensitive manufacturing firms, schools, civic buildings, and housing for people of various income levels, all within a mixed-use, walkable community connected to the greater region via public transit (light-rail, bus, and commuter van). The development includes other essential features of a sustainable garden city, including recreational amenities such as an outdoor entertainment center, organic farming, habitat protection, green building, and recycling of water and wastes.

This groundbreaking project was spearheaded by a visionary, dedicated, and enthusiastic developer. Clark's environmental goals for the project included acknowledging nature and accepting environmental responsibility. Among his social goals were respecting and involving residents, providing sites for civic life of the community, and avoiding economic segregation.

The Haymount design process was exemplary. Clark studied the site using geographic information systems (GIS) mapping. All trees sixteen inches in diameter or larger were mapped, along with habitats of 302 animal species, vegetation types, wildlife corridors, and wetlands. The land's archaeological past was studied. Through this process, areas were identified that could be developed with minimal disruption of the site's natural ecosystems. Clark was also committed to a thorough and inclusive planning process and held numerous meetings and design workshops, inviting community groups, local church members, and representatives of local and regional government agencies to attend. Clark promoted the idea of a multicultural community and reached out to the area's residents, who are predominantly African American. As a result, the local communities supported his efforts, and three churches openly backed his project.

Haymount consists of 4,000 residential units for people of various income levels, 500,000 square feet of office and light industrial space, 250,000 square feet of retail space, and a fifty-acre college campus, all organized according to new urbanist principles. Almost 70 percent of the site is being preserved in its natural state, reforested, or maintained as productive organic farmland.

The community incorporates the largest biological wastewater treatment system proposed to date as well as a storm-water management system that employs constructed wetlands and biotechnical methods. Sewage effluent will be run through a series of translucent tanks containing plants, snails, fish, and other organisms. The tanks, along with a constructed wetland that accomplishes the final cleansing, will be housed in a greenhouse. This will serve as both wildlife habitat and a civic park. The facility is being designed to use photovoltaic fuel cells as its energy supply.

Clark initiated a "green builder" program, devising energy and materials codes to encourage and reward builders for constructing resource-efficient housing.

A portion of the site will continue to be farmed, but organic farming will replace the chemical-intensive agriculture that was practiced on the land for the previous forty years. A scheme has been devised to allow an organic farmer to lease a large block of farmland for $1 per year for thirty years. The farm will provide food for restaurants, grocery stores, and a farmers' market in the town so that Haymount residents, as well as others from the area, will be able to purchase organically grown produce and support local sustainable agriculture.

Because it is located away from the freeway corridor and along a pristine river, Haymount has been criticized and its approvals aggressively challenged by owners of adjacent land for being "the right plan in the wrong place." Their fear is that the development will attract sprawl and encroach on the surrounding farmland. However, although Haymount may not be located in the best place from a regional perspective, it does represent a vastly superior alternative to the ten-acre "martini farms" for which the area was previously zoned.

Clark was challenged by the county's Department of Planning and Community Development to propose ways to prevent sprawl in Caroline County from following in Haymount's wake. His attorney, Dan Slone, developed language for the river corridor that designates certain areas as environmentally sensitive to ensure that improved land use patterns will minimize adverse effects of future developments spurred by Haymount.

It should be noted that innovation costs a lot of money. Particularly costly is the time and effort required to gain approval of innovations such as Haymount's radical sewage system and narrow streets. It took Clark ten years to get the development through the approval process. Although this project might correctly be criticized for its location, the reason why such an innovative project could be undertaken at all is that the site was not zoned for high-density development and was therefore available at a low price. Clark was able to convince the landowner to sell the land at its current value and to become a limited partner in the project. The property owner then could sell the land at a low price and still realize considerable profit if the project were approved.

The major investor in Haymount, the W. C. and A. N. Miller Company, was willing to provide the money needed for an extensive planning and approval process, again because of the low cost of the land. The company's executives believed that they could invest several million dollars up front and, should the project fail to get approvals, still sell the improved land under existing zoning and make a profit.

The lesson here is that although Haymount may be in the wrong place, if it were in the right place it would be financially infeasible. This will continue to be the general case until sustainable development practices receive more support from local government agencies and lending institutions.

Construction was scheduled to begin in Haymount in the fall of 1999, with a projected twenty-year build-out. It remains to be seen whether this vision will come to full fruition, but approvals are in place for the innovative features of the community, including the ecological wastewater treatment facility and community greenhouse—features for which the support of local government is often very difficult to gain. Haymount holds great promise for raising the standard of what can be accomplished in terms of sustainable development in the future.

CASE STUDY—CIVANO

Civano is an example of a garden city built on the edge of an existing city. It is located thirteen miles from downtown Tucson, Arizona, a city that lacks a strong downtown employment base. Sitting on 1,145 acres, it is planned as a walkable, resource-efficient community with high-density development around a village center, where 50 percent of the housing and 70 percent of the jobs will be located. The plan provides for a build-out of 2,600 residential units, 35 acres of commercial and retail space, more than 200 acres of open space, and a 65-acre environmental technology business park.

It was a local builder who first had the idea of building a "solar village" in Tucson. Understanding that implementing such a project would be impossible without political support, he approached Bruce Babbitt, who was then governor of Arizona. Babbitt was enthusiastic about the idea and took action, allocating oil overcharge funds to help pay for the project and identifying a large parcel of land held in state trust as the potential site. As planning progressed, the concept grew from a solar village to a larger undertaking, a community that would be economically, physically, and socially sustainable.

When local government officials realized that their city could save about $0.5 million per year in reduced costs (for long-term water treatment, road maintenance, trash disposal, and pollution abatement) if population growth in the city were accommodated in an environmentally sensitive manner, they joined the effort to create a new garden city. Over time, the entire community, including the city, the county, the state, and local citizens, also became excited about the project and took an active role in planning and developing Civano. Whereas most sustainable development projects have been initiated, financed, and carried out by innovative developers, Civano represents a new model in which government is the driving force.

Planning for Civano began in the late 1980s. The city of Tucson obtained a grant from the Urban Consortium Energy Task Force to hire a full-time project manager for the development. He was hired as a Pima County employee, paid with federal funds, and based in the city's Office of Energy and Environment. This collaborative approach has been a hallmark of Civano.

Another project participant, the Tucson–Pima County Metropolitan Energy Commission, served as an advisor. With funding from the Arizona State Energy Office, the commission solicited input from fifty different public and private groups and involved hundreds of local citizens in the planning process. Designers employed Ian McHarg's overlay methodology in planning the site.

The Civano property had to be auctioned by the Arizona State Land Department, but prior to the auction, the city of Tucson took an active role in ensuring that an appropriate developer would bid on the property, one who would carry out the project according to the city's vision. The city set clear performance standards for the development while allowing for the builder's creativity in achieving them.

To convince potential developers that the project would be commercially viable, the city surveyed 300 Tucson residents to determine whether they would be willing to pay more to live in a development with "resource conservation and community features." The survey revealed that 80 percent would pay a $5,000 to $10,000 premium for these amenities.

In 1996, the city became a financial partner in the project, promising tax-free municipal bond financing of as much as $38 million for infrastructure and a city grant of as much as $3 million for off-site infrastructure improvements and construction of the primary boulevard. Additional city funds of as much as $4 million, to be derived from general obligation bonds, were committed toward construction of the community center and park (previously planned for a site adjacent to Civano).

If Civano is a financial success, the city's $3 million general fund investment will be repaid in six years. The city will also save about $200 per unit annually in perpetuity in avoided costs of roads, potable water, and landfill development. That figure may seem modest, but it is twice the revenue to the city from the primary property tax on a typical $125,000 house. Tucson's mayor, George Miller, remarked, "Investments in smart growth yield substantial returns."

The Fannie Mae American Communities Fund has become a major equity investor in the community of Civano. Officials of Fannie Mae believe that Civano represents a new model for environmentally sensitive development, one that can be replicated around the United States as smart growth takes hold.

The developable area of the Civano project occupies 916 acres. It includes a total of 2,700 homes; 1 million square feet of commercial, office, and industrial space; a large town center; smaller neighborhood centers; and community and recreational services. One-third of the acreage will remain as open space containing orchards, parks, walking trails, bicycle paths, and a golf course.

Civano is laid out in four neighborhoods, each consisting of clusters of homes surrounding common open space. Each neighborhood has a neighborhood center at its core. Swimming pools are provided in these centers to reduce the demand for water for individual pools. The site plan of one of the neighborhoods is modeled after Village Homes; others take a new urbanist form. Neighborhoods, in turn, surround the village center. Because the automobile has been declared second in importance to the pedestrian and bicyclist, numerous pedestrian linkages are planned, and a community tram is a future goal.

The project blends resource efficiency and neotraditional design elements, with the goal of reducing energy demand by 75 percent, water use by 65 percent, solid waste by 90 percent, and automobile-generated air pollution by 40 percent. To help achieve these goals, minimum standards require builders to construct homes that use half the energy and potable water of typical structures. A "green builder" program is implemented by educating builders, developers, residents, and the community about sustainable building techniques.

Civano's buildings will be equipped with high-efficiency insulation and

The first neighborhood center to be built in Civano, a garden city on the outskirts of Tucson. (Photograph courtesy of the city of Tucson, Arizona)

water and solid waste systems. Overhangs will shade windows from the hot summer sun. Indigenous building materials and building designs are flourishing. Builders are also encouraged to keep duct distribution systems inside buildings and to install energy-efficient appliances and solar water-heating systems. All irrigation must be accomplished without the use of potable water—a reclaimed water system is available to all properties, the first such system in a new development in Tucson. Together, these strategies will enable builders to downsize the houses' heating, cooling, and ventilation systems, and this will save enough money to significantly offset the costs of the efficiency measures.

Civano will be relatively affordable and will cover the entire middle of the Tucson market. Five regional builders are constructing the homes, providing a diversity of housing types. Consumer response to all housing types has been strong.

The project's manager, John Laswick, noted that cutting monthly utility costs by $35 to $40 allows residents to pay as much as $5,000 more for the homes without changing their total monthly cost. He observed that this increases equity in the home rather than utility company profits.

Homes in Civano reflect historic architectural patterns and are highly energy efficient. (Photograph courtesy of the city of Tucson, Arizona)

Businesses locating in Civano are expected to create one job for every two homes. A sixty-five-acre environmental technology business park is already home to a manufacturer of photovoltaic panels. The landscape firm that salvaged native plants from the construction site has opened a commercial nursery and set up a center to teach the public about desert vegetation.

Civano's grand opening took place in April 1999, with Arizona's governor, Jane Dee Hull, hailing the development as the "poster child for better planning." As of this writing, the first homes were under construction in Civano, with 200 scheduled to be completed by the end of 1999. Construction was complete on the first neighborhood center, where 20,000 square feet of retail space has been preleased for such uses as a café, a gallery, a print shop, and office space. The entire development is expected to be completed by 2009.

CASE STUDY—COFFEE CREEK CENTER

Coffee Creek Center is planned as a sustainable garden city and serves as an extension to the town of Chesterton, Indiana, a community with a population of 10,000. The development's 640-acre master plan calls for a pedestrian-oriented community made up of several mixed-use neighborhoods and

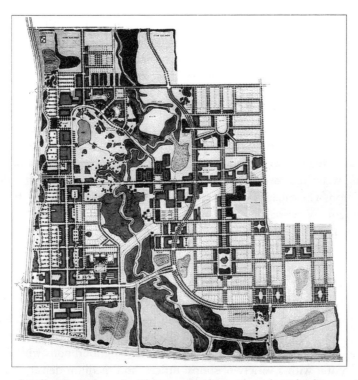

A map of Coffee Creek Center in Chesterton, Indiana, shows how development is integrated with a natural area. (Figure courtesy of William McDonough and Partners)

a "main street" commercial area, 185 acres of restored natural habitat, and about 230 acres of parks and greens. A total of about 1,350 residential units and 3 million square feet of commercial, office, and retail space is planned. Some light industrial uses may also be incorporated.

In 1981, the town of Chesterton annexed the site to help shape the path of future development. The property was acquired in 1995 by the current developer, the Lake Erie Land Company. The company hired visionary architect William McDonough—named a "hero of the planet" by *Time* magazine—to set forth the project's environmental planning and building principles. These include minimizing the use of nonrenewable resources, reusing and recycling materials, and using sustainably harvested materials wherever practical. Buildings are to be oriented to take advantage of the sun and wind, and photovoltaic electric generation and other advanced energy systems are planned. State-of-the-art communication and data systems are also to be incorporated.

Water is to be treated as a resource, not a waste product. All storm water will eventually be absorbed using techniques such as rooftop retention, "green" roofs (roofs that have plantings on them), swales planted with native water-loving vegetation, dry wells, cisterns, continuous tree-planting trenches, wetlands, and perforated pipes. Ongoing testing has been carried out to determine the effectiveness of each. This has led to installation of a "leaky pipe" system, which allows runoff water that falls on the built portion of the development to be funneled through a series of pipes with holes in them, allowing the water to leak out slowly. There are four series of pipes, allowing water that overflows the first to run into the next, one foot lower in elevation. The capacity of this system far exceeds the output of a 100-year storm event. Water passing through it is cleansed of toxins before it reaches the stream, and the stream is kept at more constant levels, preventing erosion along its banks.

The sewage system will remove solids, and effluent will flow through constructed wetlands like those in the city of Arcata, California, described in chapter 6. Indoor biological treatment systems may also be used.

The master plan provides for neotraditional neighborhoods located on either side of a central open space and creek, with a path system connecting common areas throughout the site. One of the neighborhoods will serve as a town center with a variety of shops, offices, and medium-density housing for "in-town" living. Immediately accessible to the exit from the Indiana Toll Road, the town center will focus on a regional customer base.

Several mixed-use residential neighborhoods will provide housing for people of a variety of income levels on narrow, tree-lined streets dotted with neighborhood parks. Neighborhood centers will provide a convenience store and other services within walking distance of the residents.

An advanced transportation system has been planned to provide door-to-door service. During off-peak hours, the system will deliver packages such as groceries and dry cleaning so that people can walk to and from their destinations without being burdened.

Landscaping is planned as a rich, attractive garden of native plants, wildflowers, and trees to minimize the need to mow, fertilize, and irrigate. Decorative yards will be minimized in favor of functional courtyards, parks, and shared outdoor space.

This project is still in the very early stages of development. The creek and the areas surrounding it are currently being restored, and three and one-half miles of a nine-mile trail system running through an area of prairie restoration are now in place. A pavilion, constructed largely by students of a nearby vocational school, has been completed using native Indiana limestone and sustainably harvested wood. Plans for three of the four development phases have been approved, and 165 miles of fiber-optic cable have been installed with the infrastructure on the site, ensuring that Coffee Creek Center's residents and businesses will enjoy the advantages of the latest technology.

City approvals were obtained in two years despite lawsuits by, ironically, an environmental group. The secret of success was a supportive town council and the legal ability in Indiana to zone for a planned unit development. This allowed the project to be approved as a whole rather than having to comply with individual city ordinances disallowing such elements as narrow streets, mixed uses, "granny flats" above garages, and shared parking. Modifications to the conventional code related to parking have in themselves saved more than forty acres in Coffee Creek Center's first phase. This land has been dedicated to a village green with substantial outdoor civic space.

One planning commission member commented, "If it works, it's great. If it doesn't, where's the harm? The alternative is more sprawl." We believe that Coffee Creek Center represents a laudable alternative to piecemeal planning. The project ensures that new growth in the city will be planned and built as an integrated set of sustainable neighborhoods.

Case Study—Davisville

Davisville is a garden city proposed for development on the other side of an interstate highway from the bulk of the city of Davis and the University of California property. Its location allows Davisville to stand alone, separated from the rest of Davis by the highway, preserved farmlands, and a creek channel. However, the community has the unique benefit of being physically closer to downtown Davis and the university campus than are many existing areas of the city. Thus, residents of this garden city will be able to reach the campus, downtown Davis, and the regional rail station through bicycle and pedestrian undercrossings.

The Davis City Council resolved in 1988, when Michael was mayor, that once the city's population reached its desired size—approximately 76,000—new growth should be located elsewhere, in what would eventually become a new city. Davis has now reached that size. Davisville has the advantage of providing housing and services for the growing University of California campus without forcing the city of Davis to grow beyond its desired population level.

Davisville is envisioned as a complete community that will combine the charming and nostalgic characteristics of new urbanist planning with the environmentally friendly concepts embodied in sustainable design. The site occupies 937 acres and will include a mixture of uses to provide a full range

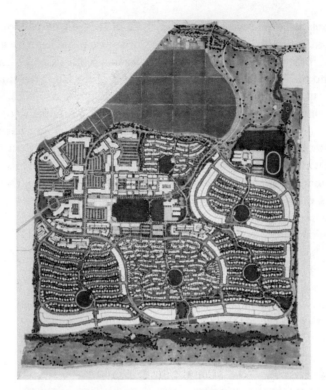

The proposed garden city of Davisville, Calfornia, will be very compact in order to conserve agricultural land.

of jobs, housing, retail services, entertainment facilities, and schools. The community is designed to reduce automobile use by means of twenty-six acres of greenbelts running through the development to connect destinations and make them easily accessible by biking and walking. It will be compact enough to be served by a bus system with transit stops within easy walking distance.

Davisville's 1,800 single-family homes and 800 apartments will be grouped in a series of neighborhoods modeled after Village Homes. All residential units, the schools, and the buildings in the town center will be oriented for solar access and natural cooling. Buildings and landscaping will, where needed, double as windbreaks and sound breaks. Food-producing trees, shrubs, vines, and gardens will be used instead of ornamental landscaping, and orchards and vineyards will be scattered throughout the project.

The town center will have a child-care center, a fire station, an athletic club, retail and office space with apartments above it, and a village green. An eighty-eight-acre business park will be located at the northern edge. Natural drainage will be used in the commercial as well as the residential areas. Parking for the business park will be provided in a walnut orchard. The community's sewage wastewater will be recycled and will serve as a source of nutrients for the landscape and for agricultural production.

Well more than one-third of the site will be dedicated to open space. A seventy-eight-acre grove of oak woodlands will be preserved. To preserve the view of these woodlands from the freeway and make a distinct border between Davis and Davisville, more than 100 acres of adjacent farmland will be dedicated to permanent cultivation. In addition, a ten-acre forest will form a visual buffer from the highway and other development on the far side of the site.

A historic ranch house and auxiliary structures, many dating back to the 1800s, will be preserved in a museum of early California agriculture. A seventy-six-acre wildlife preserve will be restored along the creek.

Davisville provides a model of what a community can do when it has reached its desired maximum size. If a town sets a growth limit and it still appears that there are economic reasons for future growth and if the region can accommodate growth, the question should not be whether to allow the town to grow beyond the optimum size but whether to establish a new garden city or garden village in an ecologically sound way, developing a separate community next to the existing one or a short distance away. Buffered from the existing city of Davis, Davisville will be just such a new town, one that can accommodate the growth pressures created by the university. We believe that this is a better alternative than continuing the current peripheral development, which has been accommodating population growth but which seems to be undermining the city's former strong sense of identity and pride.

The New Garden Village Neighborhood

Ideally, a new garden village should be planned as part of a garden city. However, in areas where master planning of this sort has not occurred, the garden village still offers social and ecological benefits.

CASE STUDY—PRAIRIE CROSSING

Prairie Crossing, located outside Chicago, serves as an example of a garden village neighborhood. Located in Grayslake, Illinois, it is primarily a residential community consisting of a total of 677 acres, with more than 65 percent of the acreage dedicated to farmland, prairies, and other open space. Commercial development is planned for the future.

The owners of Prairie Holdings Corporation, the developer of Prairie Crossing, are neighbors of the site and longtime residents of the area who passionately wished to preserve the region's historical landscape—a combination of prairies, farmland, wetlands, and trees. A plan for developing more than 1,600 homes had been stopped through court proceedings when Prairie Holdings Corporation stepped in, bought the property, and proposed instead a "conservation community" with 317 homes built in clusters and the rest of the property preserved as open space. None of the eight families involved had any previous experience in development; however, all of them felt sure that a developer could do better-quality development and still make money.

The leaders of the development corporation, Victoria and George Ranney Jr., set forth clear goals for the development. These include protection and enhancement of the environment, economic viability, economic and racial diversity, and a healthy lifestyle that includes a sense of community. In an interview, Victoria Ranney said, "What we wanted to do is make a conservation community that would allow people to live on the land in ways that enhance their lives and the land itself."

The development was sited around existing hedgerows, wetlands, and other terrain. The housing stock consists entirely of single-family homes organized in four neighborhoods: a neotraditional cluster of homes with a market square and a village green; prairie homes clustered in groups of eight with views of open prairie; meadow homes with landscaped common areas overlooking marshes, lakes, or fields; and field homes that border farm fields or pastures viewed through hedgerows.

In 1998, housing prices at Prairie Crossing ranged from $194,000 to $409,000. The homes, which can be chosen from a selection of sixteen different styles, are very well insulated and feature energy-efficient appliances and lighting. These features have reduced energy consumption by 50 percent compared with other homes in the area. Built-in cabinets provide bins for recycling. Low-flush toilets and faucet aerators cut water use. Even with up-to-date amenities, the homes retain the historic style of Midwest homesteads.

New residents are educated about the merits of landscaping with native species rather than the typical lawn, and about 60 percent of them now dedicate at least a portion of their yard to natives. A monthly newsletter, a handbook, and seminars help homeowners identify native species and manage their plantings.

A historic barn, a schoolhouse, and a farmhouse have been preserved. The barn serves as a community center, and the schoolhouse is used for the

Prairie Crossing, a garden village neighborhood near Chicago, preserves 65 percent of the site as open space. (Figure courtesy of Victoria Ranney)

lower grades of a charter elementary school. The guiding principles for Prairie Crossing state, "The community buildings—an historic barn, a schoolhouse and a farmhouse—remind us that others have lived on this land before, and that others, to whom we have responsibility, will live here after us."

A train stop adjacent to the site provides service to the downtown area and the airport. A compact retail, office, and residential area is planned for development around the rail stop, according to developer Victoria Ranney.

Homes in Prairie Crossing are state-of-the-art in energy efficiency while reflecting the historic prairie style. (Photograph courtesy of Victoria Ranney)

About 75 acres of land outside the residential development is being held for future light industrial or commercial use.

The development company saved $1.4 million in infrastructure costs by using narrower streets and natural storm-water drainage. Runoff is routed through a series of swales into reconstructed prairie and wetlands before flowing into a 22-acre artificial lake. This surface flow allows the water to be held long enough in different microenvironments to increase absorption into the ground. The system also removes 98 percent of the pollutants picked up by the storm water before it reaches the lake. This allows the lake to be used for swimming and stocked with native endangered fish species.

Of the 150 acres of farmland in the community, to date 14 acres are devoted to a certified organic community-supported garden. About 100 families are members of the garden, which is managed by a couple living on-site. Members may work in the garden and go there to pick up about ten pounds of produce per week throughout the twenty-week growing season. A Saturday farmers' market held during the growing season serves as another outlet for the produce and as a community gathering place. A stable and pastures for residents with horses and small farm animals sit on 25 acres. The balance of the 150 acres of farmland is leased to a farmer, who grows corn and soybeans; this land will eventually be converted to organic production. The Conservation Fund, based in Arlington, Virginia, holds an easement that will preserve the 150 acres as open land in perpetuity.

Additional open space, a total of 310 acres, is used for reconstructed prairie, hedgerows, and trails for walking, bicycling, and horseback riding. A number of animal species are now in residence, including egrets, herons, chorus frogs, butterflies, geese, and other wildlife.

Since the first house was sold, in December 1994, 132 families have moved into Prairie Crossing, and construction is under way on another thirty-five lots. One-half percent of the proceeds from each home sale goes to support the Liberty Prairie Foundation for environmental education and stewardship programs.

Residents of Prairie Crossing have developed a strong sense of community, probably because the opportunities to interact are numerous. Neighbors encounter one another while picking up food at the community-supported garden, on the trails, and at the playing fields and the barn—the site of dances, potluck suppers, meetings, wedding receptions, concerts, and the like.

The developers of Prairie Crossing have proven, as have we in Village Homes, that it is possible to make money while designing with nature for people. The project is on track to make its projected 6 to 8 percent profit on the $100 million development cost.

The Garden City in Urban Revitalization

In addition to addressing new development, the concept of garden cities offers existing communities a planning tool to facilitate urban remodeling. First steps have been taken that make the path to creating garden cities through urban revitalization seem achievable.

The Miami-based architectural firm of Dover, Kohl & Partners has held workshops with the residents of numerous neighborhoods in need of revitalization to develop plans to make them more walkable and more enjoyable places to live. They often use computer simulation so that participants can see what their plan will look like when it is built. Generally, these workshops are initiated and funded by local governments.

A recent Dover-Kohl project involved the transformation of an old mall located in a declining inner suburban ring of Chattanooga, Tennessee, into a town center. The project was initiated by the city. The city staff raised money by convincing owners of businesses in and around the dying mall to

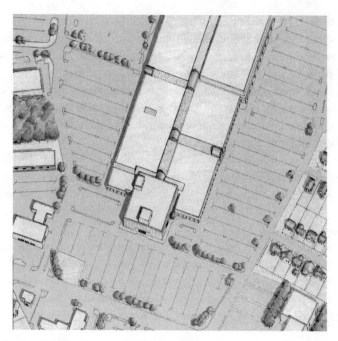

The architectural firm of Dover, Kohl & Partners started with a typical mall in Chattanooga, Tennessee, that looks like many others throughout the country. (Figure courtesy of Dover, Kohl & Partners)

cover 80 percent of the cost of a plan to revitalize the mall. They then hired Dover-Kohl and transportation engineer Walter Kulash as the design team.

The design team engaged 300 people, including nearby residents and business owners, in the design process. One hundred fifty community members did the core of the work, breaking into groups to create separate plans for the area. These were evaluated by the rest of the participants and combined to form a composite draft plan. The plan that the group came up with is a highly innovative one that will, over time, transform the mall into a town center.

Initially, the mall's owners were not particularly excited about the process, but when they saw the vision and enthusiasm of nearby residents and businesses, they "got hooked." The plan, backed by the mall's owners, the city, residents, and other businesses in the area, calls for turning the mall inside out. A new road will cut the existing building in half, embedding it in a street grid with new office, retail, and residential construction. The mall's exterior will be refaced with new outward-facing storefronts. Much of the

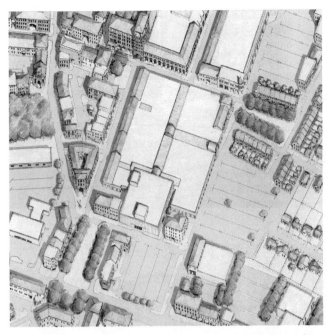

The first step will be to divide the mall's structure in half and replace some of the asphalt parking area with other uses. (Figure courtesy of Dover, Kohl & Partners)

existing fifty acres of surface parking will become parks, housing, civic buildings, and a town square. A hotel is also proposed.

Victor Dover of Dover-Kohl said that he believes it is critical that local governments take the initiative on such projects: "With a variety of property owners, the only common manager of the whole process is the community, the city. That's why the city is involved in the planning, because no one else is responsible for the big picture."[1]

The Dover-Kohl process in Chattanooga could easily be replicated by other local governments to facilitate further remodeling of urban areas into garden cities or garden villages. An important component of such efforts would be to educate citizen design participants about additional concepts that could be incorporated in their plans, such as community gardens and solar water heaters, as was done in the Civano new garden city project. The American Institute of Architects, based in Washington, D.C., published a workbook in 1996 that could help. The *Environmental Design Charrette Workbook* gives guidance on how to address energy efficiency, building technology, environmental approaches to landscaping, waste prevention, and

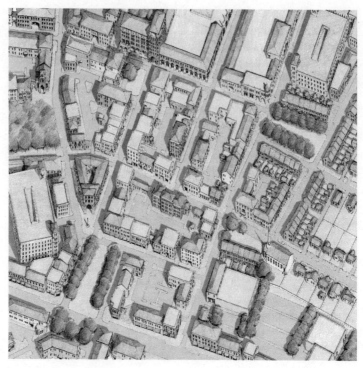

The final goal is to transform the mall into an attractive town center. (Figure courtesy of Dover, Kohl & Partners)

A lovely town square will cover up any trace of the former Chattanooga mall. (Figure courtesy of Dover, Kohl & Partners)

resource reclamation, as well as planning and cultural issues, through the charette process (an intense workshop in which all the stakeholders gather to complete a plan within a concentrated period of time).

The case studies documented in this chapter illustrate that the transition to more sustainable development is within our reach. We must appreciate the efforts of those developers, builders, private and public planners and architects, engineers, financiers, local government leaders and their staffs, and others who have made these projects possible. The key to future success lies in our ability to enlighten the vast majority whose professional efforts are still contributing to piecemeal planning, cookie-cutter design, and urban sprawl.

Local elected officials and planners must recognize an environmentally sound development when they see one and be willing to be flexible and innovative in supporting it. They must be willing to be proactive in planning to ensure that new development is more sustainable rather than just responding to piecemeal proposals. Finally, they must take the lead in the redesign of existing communities.

The development industry must also be willing to change. This may be the most difficult task ahead. But given the public response to the forward-looking projects discussed in this book, the industry members who do step forward will reap equal if not greater rewards for their efforts.

We are thankful that the momentum is starting to shift to more ecologically sound development. The health and sustainability of the earth as a whole and our individual local communities will depend on this momentum, in a chain reaction, coming fully into blossom. Sustainable community building must not be the rarity but rather business as usual.

Notes

Chapter 1: From Piecemeal Planning to Sustainable Development

1. P. Schiller, "Green Streets," *Progress* (newsletter of the Surface Transportation Policy Project, Washington, D.C.) (June 1997), 4.
2. M. Orfield, *Metropolitics* (Washington, D.C.: Brookings Institution, 1997).
3. R. Dubos, *Beast or Angel: Choices That Make Us Human* (New York: Charles Scribner's Sons, 1974), 92.
4. E. Howard, *Garden Cities of Tomorrow* (1898; reprint, Cambridge, Mass.: MIT Press, 1965), 192.
5. C. Sussman, ed., *Planning the Fourth Migration: The Neglected Vision of the Regional Planning Association of America* (Cambridge, Mass.: MIT Press, 1976), 45.
6. C. Stein, *Toward New Towns for America* (Cambridge, Mass.: MIT Press, 1989).
7. *Changed Travel—Better World* (London: TEST, 1991), 11.
8. E. F. Schumacher, *Small Is Beautiful: Economics as if People Mattered* (New York: Harper & Row, 1973).
9. H. T. Odum, *Environment, Power, and Society* (New York: Wiley-Interscience, 1971).
10. E. T. Hall, *The Hidden Dimension* (New York: Doubleday & Company, 1966).
11. R. Sommer, *Personal Space: The Behavioral Basis of Design* (Englewood Cliffs, N.J.: Prentice-Hall, 1969).
12. R. Sommer, *Social Design: Creating Buildings with People in Mind* (Englewood Cliffs, N.J.: Prentice-Hall, 1983).
13. A. T. Lovins, *Soft Energy Paths: Toward a Durable Peace* (San Francisco: Friends of the Earth International, 1977; distributed by Ballinger Publishing Company, Cambridge, Mass.).
14. A hectare is equivalent to 2.47 acres.
15. M. Thompson-Fawcett, "The Urbanist Revision of Development," *Urban Design International* 1, no. 4 (1996): 301–322.

16. D. Kelbaugh, ed., *The Pedestrian Pocket Book: A New Suburban Design Strategy* (New York: Princeton Architectural Press in association with the University of Washington, 1989).

17. P. Katz, *The New Urbanism* (New York: McGraw-Hill, 1994).

18. M. Winogrond, "Reweaving California's Cities: Principles of Livable Communities," *Western City* (Sacramento, Calif.) 73, no. 3 (March 1997): 5–8.

19. *Livable Places Update* (newsletter of the Local Government Commission, Center for Livable Communities, Sacramento, Calif.) (June 1996).

20. R. Steuteville, "Year of Growth for New Urbanism," *New Urban News*, no. 5 (1998): 1, 3–7.

21. U.S. Department of Housing and Urban Development, *Principles for Designing and Planning Homeownership Zones*, HUD-1612-CPD (Washington, D.C.: U.S. Department of Housing and Urban Development, Office of Community Planning and Development, July 1996).

22. Urban Land Institute, *ULI on the Future: Smart Growth* (Washington, D.C.: Urban Land Institute, 1998).

23. S. Cowan and S. Van der Ryn, *Ecological Design* (Washington, D.C.: Island Press, 1996).

24. R. Thayer, *Gray World, Green Heart: Technology, Nature, and Sustainable Landscape* (New York: John Wiley & Sons, 1994).

25. T. Beatley and K. Manning, *The Ecology of Place: Planning for Environment, Economy, and Community* (Washington, D.C.: Island Press, 1997).

26. R. Ewing, *Best Development Practices: A Primer for Smart Growth* (Washington, D.C.: American Planning Association, 1998).

27. Rocky Mountain Institute, *Green Development: Integrating Ecology and Real Estate* (New York: John Wiley & Sons, 1998).

28. M. Leccese, "A Growing Concern in Colorado's Front Range," *Urban Land* (Urban Land Institute, Washington, D.C.) (April 1998), 8.

29. President's Council on Sustainable Development, *Building on Consensus: A Progress Report on Sustainable America* (Washington, D.C.: President's Council on Sustainable Development, 1997).

30. Speech delivered Monday, January 11, at the American Institute of Architects building in Washington, D.C.

31. Bank of America, *Beyond Sprawl: New Patterns of Growth to Fit the New California* (San Francisco: Bank of America, 1995).

32. S. Levy, *Land Use and the California Economy* (San Francisco: Californians and the Land, 1998).

Chapter 2: An Introduction to Village Homes

1. D. Jackson, "Back to the Garden: A Suburban Dream," *Time*, 22 February 1999.

2. H. Reese, personal communication, February 1994.

3. J. Hamrin, "Two Energy Conserving Communities: Implications for Public Policy" (Ph.D. diss., University of California, Davis, 1978).

Chapter 3: The Basis for Sustainable Development

1. R. Erdoes and L. Deer, *Seeker of Visions* (New York: Touchstone Books/Simon and Schuster Trade, 1973).
2. R. Margalef, *Perspectives in Ecological Theory* (Chicago: University of Chicago Press, 1970); H. Odum, *Environment, Power, and Society* (New York: Wiley-Interscience, 1971).
3. Margalef, *Perspectives in Ecological Theory.*
4. A. Maslow, *Motivation and Personality* (New York: Harper, 1954).
5. R. Dubos, *Beast or Angel: Choices That Make Us Human* (New York: Charles Scribner's Sons, 1974), 157.
6. *Take Back Your Streets: How to Protect Communities from Asphalt and Traffic* (Boston: Conservation Law Foundation, May 1995).
7. *Livable Places Update* (newsletter of the Local Government Commission, Center for Livable Communities, Sacramento, Calif.) (May 1998).
8. M. Bookchin, *The Limits of the City* (New York: Harper & Row, 1974), 124.
9. C. Bragdon, *Noise Pollution: The Unquiet Crisis* (Philadelphia: University of Pennsylvania Press, 1970).
10. R. Baron, *The Tyranny of Noise* (New York: St. Martin's Press, 1970).
11. Ibid., 54.

Chapter 4: Water, Food, Shelter: The Basics

1. R. Sabin, "How to Choose Crops to Water," *San Francisco Chronicle,* 4 March 1991, C-1.
2. B. A. Cohen, R. Wiles, E. D. Olson, and C. Campbell, *Just Add Water: Violations of Federal Health Standards in Tap Water* (Washington, D.C.: Environmental Working Group and Natural Resources Defense Council, May 1996), 1.
3. U.S. Fish and Wildlife Service, "Listed Proposed and Candidate Species in Northern and Central California," 10 February 1999.
4. D. Conrad, *Higher Ground* (Vienna, Va.: National Wildlife Federation, 1998).
5. Metropolitan Water District of Southern California, *Southern California's Integrated Water Resources Plan,* vol. 1, *The Long-Term Resources Plan* (Los Angeles: Metropolitan Water District of Southern California, March 1996).
6. Internet: <http://www.treepeople.org/trees>.
7. P. Martineau, "What's Water Recycling? County to Explain," *Sacramento Bee,* 17 April 1999, Metro 1 and 5.
8. M. Hollis (Metropolitan Water District of Southern California), personal communication, April 1999.

9. *South Carolina Coastal Conservation League Land Development Bulletin* (Charleston, S.C.), no. 7 (fall 1995).

10. R. Barnet, "The World's Resources, Part II—Minerals, Food, and Water," *New Yorker,* 31 March 1980, 91.

11. U.S. Department of Agriculture, *Report and Recommendation on Organic Farming Science and Education Administration,* annual report (Washington, D.C.: U.S. Department of Agriculture, 1980).

12. California Department of Water Resources, *California Water Plan Update,* Bulletin no. 160-93 (Sacramento: California Department of Water Resources, October 1994).

13. Gunter Redlin (supervising sanitary engineer, California State Department of Health, Sanitary Engineering Section, Fresno, California), personal communication.

14. U.S. Department of Agriculture, *Report and Recommendation.*

15. Rick Martin (general manager, South San Joaquin Irrigation District), personal communication, May 1998.

16. R. Blobaum, "Using Organic Agriculture in Sustainable Development," *In Business* (Emmaus, Pa.) 19, no. 6 (November–December 1997): 12–13.

17. Ibid.

18. *The Food Miles Report: The Dangers of Long-Distance Food Transport* (London: SAFE Alliance, October 1992).

19. A. Arnett, "Growth Industries," *Boston Globe Magazine,* 28 September 1997.

20. E. Streich, personal communication.

Chapter 5: Society's Lifeblood: Energy

1. J. Fowler, *Energy-Environment Source Book* (Washington, D.C.: National Science Teachers Association, 1975).

2. C. Flavin and N. Lenssen, *Power Surge: Guide to the Coming Energy Revolution* (New York: W. W. Norton & Company, 1994).

3. C. Moore, *Dying Needlessly: Sickness and Death Due to Energy-Related Air Pollution* (College Park, Md.: Renewable Energy Policy Project, 1997), 24.

4. A. Lovins, *Soft Energy Paths: Toward a More Durable Peace* (Cambridge, Mass.: Ballinger Publishing Company, 1977), 59.

5. D. Hayes, *Rays of Hope: The Transition to a Post-Petroleum World* (New York: W. W. Norton & Company, 1977), 27–28.

6. J. Berger, *Charging Ahead: The Business of Renewable Energy and What It Means for America* (New York: Henry Holt & Company, 1997).

7. D. Hayes, *Worldwatch Paper II—Energy: The Solar Prospect* (Washington, D.C.: Worldwatch Institute, March 1977).

8. D. Bainbridge, J. Corbett, and J. Hofacre, *Village Homes' Solar House Designs* (Emmaus, Pa.: Rodale Press, 1979).

9. G. Luft, "Small Hydro: Part of the Energy Answer," *Reclamation Era* 65, no. 1 (1979): 20.

10. M. Harris, "Reinventing the Waterwheel," *Environmental Action* 11, no. 1 (June 1979): 24.

11. U.S. Department of Commerce, *Residential Energy Uses,* Pamphlet no. 003-024-01554-4 (Washington, D.C.: U.S. Government Printing Office, 1975).

12. J. Ridgeway and C. S. Projansky, *Energy-Efficient Community Planning: A Guide to Saving Energy and Producing Power at the Local Level* (Emmaus, Pa.: JG Press, 1979).

13. L. Bazdur, "Geothermal Energy for Space and Process Heating," in *Energy Technology Handbook,* ed. D. M. Considine (New York: McGraw-Hill, 1975).

14. J. Fowler, *Energy and the Environment* (New York: McGraw-Hill, 1975).

15. J. Todd and N. Todd, *Tomorrow Is Our Permanent Address* (New York: Harper & Row, 1980), 52.

16. G. B. Arrington Jr., *At Work in the Field of Dreams: Light Rail and Smart Growth in Portland* (Portland: Tri-County Metropolitan Transportation District of Oregon (Tri-Met), 1998).

17. B. Commoner, *The Politics of Energy* (New York: Alfred A. Knopf, 1979), 49.

Chapter 6: The Use of Resources in Sustainable Design

1. R. Barnet, "The World's Resources, Part III—Human Energy," *New Yorker,* 7 April 1980, 109.

2. R. Barnet, "The World's Resources, Part II—Minerals, Food, and Water," *New Yorker,* 31 March 1980, 59.

3. W. Goldschmidt, *Small Business and the Community: A Study in the Central Valley of California on the Effects of Scale of Farm Operations,* Report of the Special Committee to Study the Problems of American Small Business, U.S. Senate, 79th Congress, 2nd session, Pursuant to S. Res. 28, 23 December 1946 (Washington, D.C.: U.S. Government Printing Office, 1946).

4. D. MacCannell, "Report on Current Social Conditions in the Communities in and near the Westlands Water District," working draft (Davis: University of California, Applied Behavioral Sciences Department, California Macrosocial Accounting Project, 1980).

5. R. Sommer, "Direct Marketing: Point/Counterpoint," *Western Fruit Grower* (February 1980): 10–11.

6. R. Cole, T. Kelley, J. Corbett, and S. Sprowls, *The Ahwahnee Principles for Smart Economic Development* (Sacramento, Calif.: Local Government Commission, 1998).

7. *Livable Places Update* (newsletter of the Local Government Commission, Center for Livable Communities, Sacramento, Calif.) (October 1998).

8. D. Henton and K. Walesh, *Linking the New Economy to the Livable Community* (Palo Alto, Calif.: Collaborative Economics, 1998).

9. Cole et al., *Ahwahnee Principles for Smart Economic Development.*
10. S. Cole, "The Emergence of Treatment Wetlands," *Small Flows* (newsletter of the National Small Flows Clearinghouse, Morgantown, W.Va.) 12, no. 4 (fall 1998): 1, 6–8.
11. M. Curtius, "Town Goes with the Low Tech Flow," *Los Angeles Times,* 30 November 1998, A3 and A24.
12. Local Government Commission, *Communities Controlling Toxics: A Handbook of Policy Initiatives* (Sacramento, Calif.: Local Government Commission, 1987).
13. *The Official Recycled Products Guide* (Ogdensburg, N.Y.: Recycling Data Management Corporation).
14. Cole et al., *Ahwahnee Principles for Smart Economic Development.*
15. Ibid.
16. D. Block, "Ecoindustrial Parks Are Ready to Take Off," *In Business* (Emmaus, Pa.) 20, no. 5 (September–October 1998): 18–21.
17. U.S. Green Building Council, 110 Sutter Street, Suite 410, San Francisco, CA 94104.
18. G. Brewster, *The Ecology of Development: Integrating the Built and Natural Environments,* ULI Research Working Paper Series, Paper no. 649 (San Francisco: California Center for Land Recycling, November 1996).

Chapter 7: Location, Size, and Density

1. *Livable Places Update* (newsletter of the Local Government Commission, Center for Livable Communities, Sacramento, Calif.) (December 1998).
2. Ibid. (September–October 1994).
3. "Sierra Business Council Partners with Placer County to Protect Open Space, Provide Certainty for Developers,"*SBC News* (newsletter of the Sierra Business Council, Truckee, Calif.) (winter 1998–1999), 1.
4. L. Mumford, *The Highway and the City* (New York: Harcourt, Brace & World, 1963), 236.
5. P. Myers, "Race to Cure Sprawl Quickens," *Green Sense* (newsletter of the Trust for Public Land, San Francisco) (fall 1997), 3.
6. L. Hempel, *Sustainable Communities: From Vision to Action* (Claremont, Calif.: Claremont Graduate University, School of Politics and Economics, Department of Politics and Policy, 1998).
7. R. T. T. Forman, *Land Mosaics: The Ecology of Landscapes and Regions* (Cambridge, England: Cambridge University Press, 1997), 496.
8. E. Howard, *Garden Cities of Tomorrow* (Cambridge, Mass.: MIT Press, 1965).
9. C. Fisher, "City Lights," *American Demographics* (October 1997): 41–47.
10. C. Stein, *Toward New Towns for America* (Cambridge, Mass.: MIT Press, 1989), 16.
11. R. Ulrich, "Human Responses to Vegetation and Landscapes," *Landscape and Urban Planning* 13 (1985): 29–44.

12. J. Dwyer, E. McPherson, H. Schroeder, and R. Rowntree, "Assessing the Benefits and Costs of the Urban Forest," *Journal of Aboriculture* 18, no. 5 (1992): 227–234.
13. O. Newman, *Architectural Design for Crime Prevention* (Washington, D.C.: U.S. Government Printing Office, 1971).
14. H. H. Iltes, P. Andrews, and O. L. Loucks, "Criteria for an Optimum Human Environment," manuscript, 1967, quoted in P. Ehrlich, *The Population Bomb* (New York: Ballantine Books, 1968), 55–56.
15. *Wall Street Journal,* 21 November 1997.
16. *Livable Places Update* (June 1998).
17. M. Wackernagel and W. Rees, *Our Ecological Footprint: Reducing Human Impact on the Earth* (Philadelphia: New Society Publishers, 1996).

Chapter 8: Designing with Nature for People: A Sustainable Approach to Urban Design

1. *Sacramento Bee,* 2 July 1978.
2. K. Sale, *Human Scale* (New York: Coward, McCann & Geoghegan, 1980), 488.
3. O. Newman, *Design Guidelines for Creating Defensible Space* (Washington, D.C.: U.S. Department of Justice, Law Enforcement Assistance Administration, 1975).
4. C. Cooper, *Resident Attitudes towards the Environment at St. Francis Square, San Francisco: A Summary of the Initial Findings,* Working Paper no. 126 (Berkeley: University of California, Institute of Urban and Regional Development, July 1970).
5. *Law Enforcement Assistance Administration Newsletter* (U.S. Department of Justice, Law Enforcement Assistance Administration, Washington, D.C.) 6, no. 6 (December 1976).
6. K. Davis, "Why Good Neighbors Mean Safe Streets," *USA Weekend,* 28–30 November 1997, 16–17.
7. E. Hall, *The Hidden Dimension* (New York: Doubleday & Company, 1966).
8. U. Bronfenbrenner, "The Origins of Alienation," *Scientific Monthly* 231 (August 1974): 53–61.
9. D. Morris, *The New City-States* (Washington, D.C.: Institute for Local Self-Reliance, 1982), 21.
10. L. Mumford, *The Highway and the City* (New York: Harcourt, Brace & World, 1953), 38.
11. *Livable Places Update* (newsletter of the Local Government Commission, Center for Livable Communities, Sacramento, Calif.) (October 1998).
12. Ibid, 1.
13. J. Jacobs, *The Death and Life of Great American Cities* (New York: Random House, 1961), 165.

14. S. Weissman and J. Corbett, *Land Use Strategies for More Livable Places* (Sacramento, Calif.: Local Government Commission, 1992).

15. Ibid.

16. D. Burden, *Street Design Guidelines for Healthy Neighborhoods* (Sacramento, Calif.: Local Government Commission, 1999).

17. R. F. White, *Effects of Landscape Development on the Natural Ventilation of Buildings and Their Adjacent Area,* Research Report no. 45 (College Station: Texas A&M University System, Texas Engineering Experiment Station, March 1945).

18. J. Hammond, M. Hunt, R. Cramer, and L. Neubauer, *A Strategy for Energy Conservation* (Davis, Calif.: City of Davis, California Energy Conservation Ordinance Project, 1974).

19. Burden, *Street Design Guidelines.*

Chapter 9:   The Process of Creating Sustainable Communities

1. J. Ruskin, *The Poetry of Architecture* (New York: John Wiley & Sons, 1891).

2. R. Sommer, F. Leary, J. Summit, and M. Tirrell, "Social Benefits of Resident Involvement in Tree Planting," *Journal of Arboriculture* 20, no. 6 (1994): 323–328.

3. C. Moore, *Participation Tools for Better Land Use Planning* (Sacramento, Calif.: Local Government Commission, 1995).

4. *Livable Places Update* (newsletter of the Local Government Commission, Center for Livable Communities, Sacramento, Calif.) (March–April 1995).

5. Ibid. (November 1997).

6. *Alternative Development Standards for Sustainable Communities* (Surrey, B.C., Canada: Fraser Valley Real Estate Board, 30 April 1998).

7. Rocky Mountain Institute, *Green Development: Integrating Ecology and Real Estate* (New York: John Wiley & Sons, 1998).

Chapter 10:   The Garden City: Case Studies of Sustainable Development in Practice

1. R. Baily, "Mall Over," *Urban Land* (Urban Land Institute, Washington, D.C.) (July 1998).

About the Authors

Judy Corbett is executive director of the Local Government Commission in Sacramento, California. The commission is a membership organization of local elected officials working to improve the economic, social, and environmental sustainability of communities. Michael Corbett is the principal of Town Planners in Davis, California, a design and planning firm specializing in environmentally sustainable development. Judy and Michael planned, developed, and built Village Homes.

Index